(PRECEDING PAGE) Seahorses provide a classic example of one of the many adaptations that enable a diversity of organisms to survive in the sea. Poor swimmers, these remarkable fish use their modified tails to anchor themselves to the stems of seaweed and sea fans, where they patiently wait for their favorite food—small crustaceans—to float past.

(OPPOSITE) Thick-billed murres, often called Brunnich's guillemots, are seen in the temperate and polar regions of the northern hemisphere. These birds breed in large colonies on coastal cliffs and are gregarious throughout the year.

(ABOVE) The West Indian sea star, *Oreaster reticulatus*, ranges along the Atlantic coast of North America from Cape Hatteras to Florida. These echinoderms have anywhere from four to seven arms, all of which possess light-sensitive nerves on the ends.

(ABOVE) The giant purple jellyfish (*Pelagia*) is common in the waters off western North America. These jellyfish use their bright colors and fleshy trailings to lure curious fish into contact with the deadly stinging cells in their tentacles.

(OPPOSITE) To many snorkelers and divers, garibaldi are synonymous with the Southern California marine environment. A constant source of underwater entertainment, these curious damselfish are protected by state law.

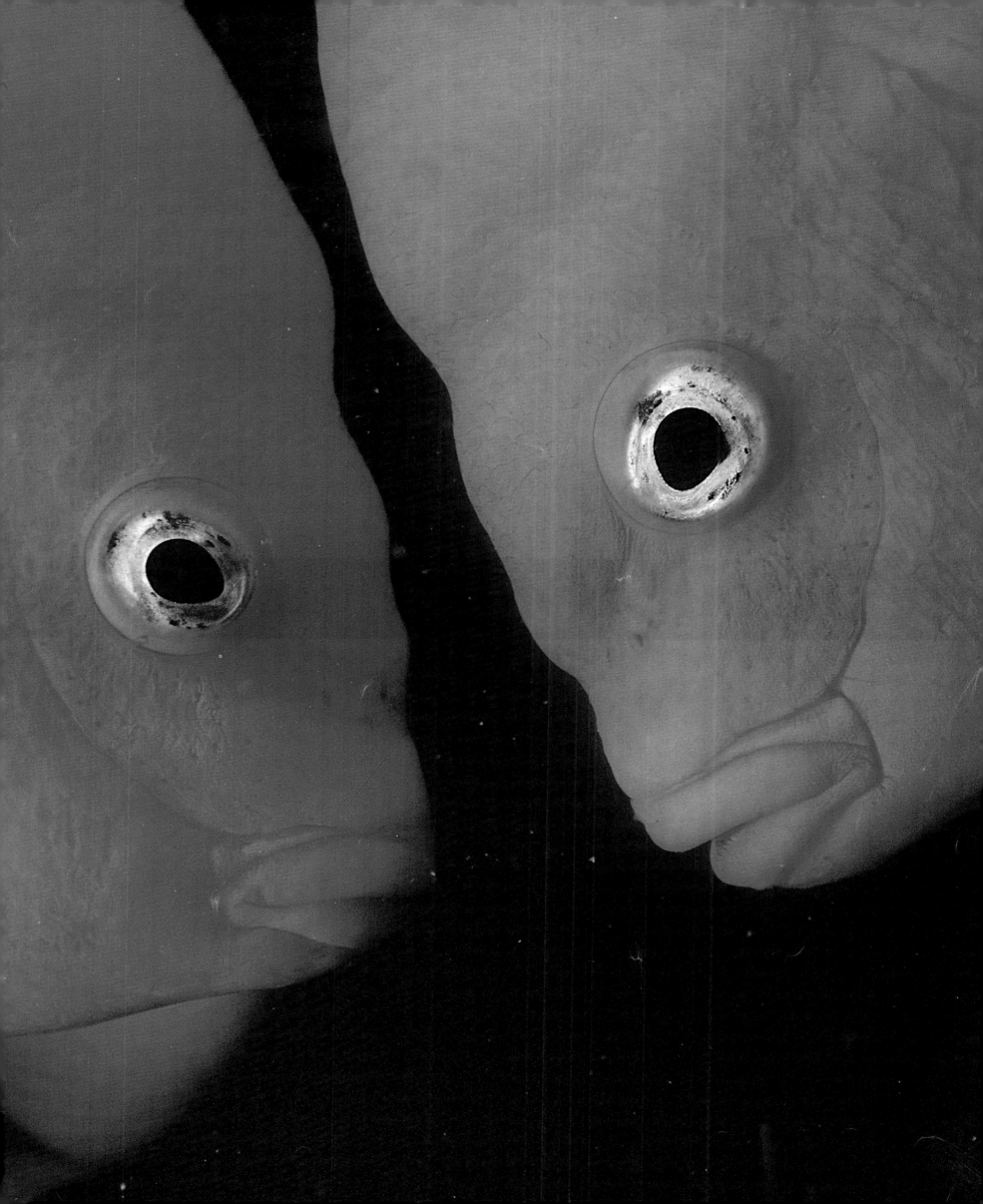

One of the most stunning of all fishes, the regal angel (*Pygoplites diacanthus*) inhabits the waters of the central, tropical Indo-Pacific. Typical of most angels, regals feed primarily on sponges.

This high-rising dorsal fin is connected to the back of the ocean's ultimate superpredator, the great white shark (*Carcharodon carcharias*). Though rare in most places, great white sharks inhabit the shallow waters of continental shelves in most temperate and tropical seas.

(FOLLOWING PAGE) Like other penguins, king penguins only stay on land to hatch and raise their offspring. After the female lays a single egg, the male will incubate it first by placing the egg between its feet and abdomen. The parents take turns during the 15-day incubation period.

The Living Oceans

MARTY SNYDERMAN

PORTLAND HOUSE

NEW YORK

This 1989 edition published by Portland House, a division of
dilithium Press, Ltd., distributed by Crown Publishers, Inc.,
225 Park Avenue South, New York, New York 10003.

Printed and Bound in Spain

ISBN 0-517-68851-4
hgfedcba

Library of Congress Cataloging in Publication Data

Snyderman, Marty
The Living Ocean / Marty Snyderman
p.   cm.
Includes index.
ISBN 0-517-68851-4
1. Marine biology.   I. Title
QH91.15.C69   1989   89-32292
574.92 – dc20   CIP

Author: Marty Snyderman

Producer: Solomon M. Skolnick
Managing Editor: Elizabeth Loonan
Designer: Barbara Cohen Aronica
Editor: Terri Hardin
Copy Editor: Richard Meyers
Production Coordinator: Ann-Louise Lipman
Picture Researcher: Edward Douglas

Foreword

Scientists have documented over 200,000 species of plants and animals that live in the world's oceans. These organisms vary in size from the tiniest single-celled plants, called diatoms, to that largest creature of all, the blue whale, that commonly reaches a length of up to 100 feet or more and can weigh more than 100 tons. And in between diatoms and great whales, there is an absolutely staggering diversity.

For human beings, however, it can be difficult to comprehend how alive the oceans really are and what life in the sea is like for the creatures who live there. One must consider the water temperature, the salinity, the depth and the amount of sunlight that penetrates into the area, the presence or lack of current, the prevailing weather conditions; whether there is a reef covered bottom, constantly shifting sand or, in the case of open sea, no bottom at all. Though it would be difficult to know these things by just standing on the beach and looking out to sea, conditions vary considerably in each of these habitats and, as a result, the plants and animals that live in these habitats can differ markedly.

It is from this perspective—the habitats within the world's oceans and the various survival adaptions of the species that live there—that this work will explore life in the sea.

Life in the Coastal Regions

Across the globe there is a considerable diversity of coastal environments, and each has its own spectrum of living conditions with which both permanent and temporary residents must contend. But is not just the presence of life along the shore that is so amazing, it is the astonishing variety of remarkable adaptations which enable survival. While mobile animals as varied as birds and crabs can simply move with the rise and fall of the tide, less mobile creatures, such as sea anemones and limpets, must be able to survive for extended periods of time both in air and underwater, as well as tolerate a wide range of constantly changing temperatures.

Coastal habitats can be generally divided into six categories: the estuaries, coastal wetlands, sandy beaches, rocky intertidal zones, subtidal benthic (or bottom) environments, and coral reef. An examination of coastal organisms, their habitats, and their coping mechanisms provides a fascinating insight into life on earth.

ESTUARIES AND COASTAL WETLANDS
Of all the oceanic habitats, many scientists maintain that estuaries are the most important in terms of human existence, but providing a strict definition of an estuary is a difficult task. In general, an estuary is a partially land-locked body of water where sea water and fresh water mix, resulting in measurably lesser amounts of salts than are found in normal sea water. They are highly fertile and productive regions, often surrounded by wetlands. These are swamp-like areas that in temperate climes are often referred to as salt marshes; in the tropics they are called mangrove swamps.

Estuaries serve as a permanent home for a wide variety of marine invertebrates and bottom-dwelling mollusks. Many birds, such as curlews, sandpipers, herons, bitterns, egrets, ibises, gulls, ducks, and geese, are also frequently seen in estuaries and marsh lands.

Turtles are common visitors. Among the estuarine turtles are hawksbill, loggerhead, and Pacific Ridley's turtle. And since estuaries link land and sea, terrestrial predators such as foxes and raccoons also search for food in these areas.

Manatees, dugongs, and sea cows (Order Sirenia) are marine animals, inhabiting shallow tropical and subtropical coastal waters along both sides of Africa, across Southern Asia and the Indo-Pacific, and in a number of locations in the western Atlantic from South America to Florida. These docile—yet voracious!—herbivores were once common from North Carolina to Florida. Today, the range of American manatees is limited to the inland waterways and rivers of central and southern Florida. In the mangrove swamps of tropical regions, mangrove trees are the dominant form of vegetation. Schooling snapper, grunts, rays, turtles, and even sharks are often seen in the shallow, yet extremely fertile waters of mangrove swamps.

SAND BEACHES
Sandy beaches are found in temperate and tropical regions around the world, wherever wave action is gentle enough to allow grains of quartz and animals skeletons to accumulate, and yet powerful enough to wash away mud, silt, and clay. The particles of sand are constantly shifting. Few plants can survive in such conditions, but a surprising number of animals manage to fare quite well.

Many of the creatures that spend significant amounts of time on and in the sand also spend extended periods of time underwater. Some smaller residents of the sand community actually move between and among the tiny grains of sand without much friction or displacement, while most larger species are excellent burrowers. The burrowers include a variety of amphipods called beach hoppers and scuds.

Common sand "fleas" are found on many sandy beaches. These creatures are actually crustaceans—not insects. Other crustaceans include a variety of crabs. Some mollusks such as California's famed Pismo clam, the wavy cockle, and the gaper clam are also found along sandy beaches. These animals are superb burrowers. Pismo clams are usually spotted by their twin siphons or siphon holes, which stand out above the sand.

Birds such as godwits, gulls, curlews, sanderlings, sandpipers, and willets probe the sand in search of a variety of amphipods and other crustaceans in the backwash of waves. Timing the outward flow of the waves, these birds often rush in and probe the just-washed sand, looking for an easy mark.

In southern California a small fish called a grunion uses the sandy beaches as a spawning ground during summer months on the second, third, and fourth nights following a full moon. The eggs are buried in the sand where they remain undisturbed for nine to eleven nights. Then, the next succession of high tides washes over the eggs. The young hatch and quickly swim out to deeper water.

THE ROCKY COASTS AND TIDE POOLS
In many areas along rocky coasts, life is evident long before you actually get to the shoreline. A skyward glance often reveals a tremendous diversity of both coastal and sea birds. In the tropics, these birds might be any of several species of frigate-birds, pelicans, terns, or gulls.

Several species of murres, gannets, and puffins breed in large colonies along some coastal cliffs in temperate regions. Far different from the expanses of gently sloping sandy beaches where the energy of waves is dissipated over a wide area, rocky shores are constantly pounded by crashing seas.

In order to cope with such demanding conditions, organisms like barnacles and chitons firmly attach themselves to rocks, while snails and hermit crabs use a strong shell for protection. Still others, like a variety of tidepool fishes, are especially adept at seeking cover in crevices between rocks. Anemones are able to retract and cover their bodies with pieces of light-colored shells and rocks in order to avoid dessication—the fatal evaporation of moisture from body tissue. Dessication is the greatest single threat to tide pool organisms.

As difficult as it might seem, many organisms flourish amid the stones and tide pools of rocky coasts. Barnacles, seaweeds, snails, and mussels vie for every available piece of real estate. Their presence attracts sea stars, fish, birds, and other predators.

Within the intertidal zone—the area that is impacted by tidal flow and spray—there is a distinct pattern of life known as vertical zonation. This definite layering of life forms found along rocky beaches is due to the differing environmental conditions. Zonation continues to some degree out beyond the tide pools into the sea, where the zones within the intertidal region are called the splash, high-tide, middle-tide, and low-tide zones. The boundaries to these zones are artificial (in that they are frequently crossed by a variety of creatures) but, in general, different organisms show strong preferences for the specific conditions of each zone.

A surprisingly high number of limpets and periwinkles (mollusks) as well as crabs, copepods, isopods, and acorn barnacles manage to live in the surf zone, with very little water, with several important species of algae.

The high-tide zone is far more populated, inhabited by a wide variety of crabs, snails, mussels, limpets, and plants.

Moving down with the ebbing tide, one enters the middle (or mid-tide) zone. The mid-tide zone is a highly competitive region. Mussels, sea stars, chitons, and barnacles compete for both space and food. The mussels combat their predators by developing thick shells and by producing more offspring that the predators can consume. If left undisturbed, mussels will usually out-compete barnacles for space on the rocks.

This zone abounds with life, such as nudibranchs. Nudibranchs, shell-less mollusks often called sea slugs, are remarkable mid-zone dwellers. Meaning "naked-gills" in Latin, the word nudibranch refers to their lack of a shell and the exposed respiratory organs which stand out on many species. However, a mere scientific description of nudibranchs does not do them justice—they are spectacular creatures. Varying from finger-nail-sized to more than a foot-long, nudibranchs appear in an incredible variety of colors and color patterns. Trying to describe a "typical" nudibranch without an accompanying photograph is an almost impossible task; they occur in many different forms, many quite bizarre-looking.

Nudibranchs are grazers, feeding on a variety of algae. As adults, they have very few predators because foul-tasting chemicals make them unappealing to potential enemies.

Diversity of species is the feature characteristic of the low-tide zone. Vertical zonation continues to a lesser extent out beyond the tide pools into the sea.

Nowhere in the world are rocky beaches more interesting than in the islands of the Galàpagos, off the west coast of Ecuador. While vertebrates are conspicuously absent from rocky beaches in most tropical habitats, cold-water species, such as Galàpagos penguins, Galàpagos fur seals and sea lions are common sights on Galàpagos shores. And marine iguanas, the only sea-going species of lizard in the world, are commonly seen in large colonies, sunning themselves on the rocks. These lizards enter the water for about an hour or so each day to feed on a variety of algaes, but when their body temperature drops too low, they quickly return to the rocks where they bask in the heat of the equatorial sun.

Life in the Rocky Reefs and Kelp Forests of Temperate Seas

In temperate regions out beyond the surf line, in areas where there is a rocky bottom, divers often encounter dense clusters of brown seaweed called kelp. In good growing conditions, many plants grow in close proximity to each other, creating stunning undersea forests called kelp beds or forests. Some forests cover up to 10 square miles.

At least 21 species of kelp can be found in California waters alone. In addition to the giant kelp that will be emphasized in this work because of its overall importance to so many creatures, the list of species includes bull kelp, palm kelps, elk kelp, and feature-boa or ribbon kelp.

Giant kelp is the ocean's largest and fastest growing plant. Individual plants attain a length of 200 feet, but that does not mean the plant grows from 200 feet deep. In fact, kelp only grows from a maximum depth of about 130 feet. The plants grow straight up off the bottom and spread out along the surface, forming a dense layer, called a canopy, which covers the forest. The canopy usually extends only 10 to 15 feet below the surface, but the canopy can be quite dense and helps to create a cathedral-like effect, as sunlight flickers through the forest like streaks of light dancing through stained glass.

With very few exceptions, kelp forests exist in areas with a rocky substrate. Mature plants consist of a holdfast, which grips the rocks below, and fronds made buoyant by a number of gas-filled bladders, called pneumatocysts. The fronds are comprised of a stem-like *stipe* (which is visually analagous to the trunk of a tree), a number of leaf-like appendages called blades, and the gas-bladders.

Kelp plants lack true roots; instead, they depend on a clump of short, thin, sturdy structures called *haptera*, which look like long pieces of spaghetti. The numerous haptera grip onto the rocks to hold the kelp plant in place. Haptera do not penetrate into the rocks like the roots of a terrestrial plant. They are well-designed to keep the plant in place in normal sea conditions; during storms, however, many plants are killed because they are pulled free of the bottom. These plants often end up on the beach, where people commonly refer to the clumps as seaweed.

Kelp, like other plants, needs sunlight to grow, and the best place to receive sunlight is at the surface. The water-tight pneumatocysts solve that problem by buoying the plant toward the surface. Unlike the vast majority of terrestrial plants where only the tops of the leaves conduct photosynthesis, both sides of the kelp blades sides to play a role in photosynthesis. Kelp plants also absorb a variety of nutrients directly out of the water through their tissues.

More than 800 species of animals are commonly found in the forests of giant kelp off the southern California coast. The giant kelp is the center of this marvelous ecosystem.

Bright orange garibaldi, curious sheepshead, schools of silver-colored jack mackerel, Catalina perch, and blacksmith fish seem omnipresent, greeting divers—almost as soon as they make a splash—on every kelp forest adventure. More than 60 species of rockfish inhabit the rocky reef below, as do moray eels, several species of colorful gobies, blennies, and sculpin. Larger migratory fishes such as yellowtail, barracuda, black seabass, and white seabass roam the kelp in search of their next meal.

Reaching a length of more than seven feet and weighing in excess of 500 pounds, giant black seabass are easily the largest commonly seen fish in kelp forests and adjacent reef communities, often inhabiting the rocky bottoms along the deeper outside edges of the forests. A host of rather diverse invertebrates inhabit the rocky reefs below the kelp. The list of abalone, rainbow-colored nudibranchs, snails, sea hares, octopi, California spiny lobsters, sea anemones, sea cucumbers, sea fans, sponges, crabs, shrimp, sea urchins, scallops, sea stars, and brittle stars is a mere sampling. It is not at all uncommon for divers to look up and see a herd of playful sea lions, a harbor seal, a school of bonito, a sea otter, or even a 50-foot-long California gray whale.

Many of the animals live their lives in very close association with the kelp. For example, kelpfish have a shape and color that makes it easy for them to hide in kelp fronds. Kelpfish mimic the kelp's movement and are superbly camouflaged. A snail, commonly called Norris' top shell, spends the majority of its life grazing on the kelp plant.

Encrusting colonies of hydroids and bryozoans take up residence on the kelp fronds. These tiny animals multiply so fast that giant kelp plants shed their blades every two to three months to prevent themselves from being over-weighted by the accumulation. Sea cucumbers lie in wait on the bottom, always ready to consume the dying kelp shed. Several species of sea urchins readily devour the plant's holdfasts, especially when competition for other foods intensifies.

The presence of these animals attracts still other creatures, such as sea otters who come to search for food. Sea otters lack the thick, protective layer of fat that helps keep other marine mammals warm in the cool waters of temperate seas. As a result, they are voracious eaters. Adults are believed to consume up to 15 percent of their body weight every day, in order to fight the effects of cold water. Sea otters are well-known for their ability to use their stubby forepaws to grasp rocks as tools, bashing abalone off of rocks and cracking open urchins and crabs.

California sea lions and harbor seals commonly cruise in the kelp and bask on the rocks at the water's edge. The underwater antics of these highly gregarious pinnipeds can entertain divers for hours. Sea lions often race in circles around divers, then stop—absolutely still in the water—hanging upside down with their whisker-covered faces only a few inches from a diver's mask. Then they suddenly race away, only to appear again within moments. Except for the bulls during their spring and summer mating season, sea lions pose very little threat and are generally welcomed by divers.

Observant divers often discover small horn and swell sharks nestled in the rocks below. They are very docile animals that prey upon small crustaceans, mollusks, echinoderms, and some fish. Leopard sharks also inhabit kelp communities.

Though not as numerous, great white sharks inhabit the kelp forests and rocky reef communities. Great whites are found throughout the tropics and in temperate seas around the world. Contrary to popular belief, they prefer to inhabit the shallow waters of continental shelves rather than the deeper waters of open ocean. Great whites live in the areas where they find large populations of prey, which often means populated stretches of coastal waters. While attacks on humans do occur, they are rare.

Occasionally a lucky diver will glance up and see a California gray whale. Gray whales are filter-feeders and certainly pose no threat, but they do attain a size of 50 feet and weigh about 50 tons. At the edges of the kelp forest, between patches of reef, the substrate is usually sand, not rock. Upon first glance, the sandy plains appear desolate and devoid of life. But upon closer inspection, divers discover a myriad of fascinating creatures. Flatfish like halibut, turbot, and sanddabs bury themselves in the sand.

Several species of octopi hunt on the sand at night. Common or market squid normally inhabit the open ocean, but during winter months they spawn over selected patches of sand. In dense spawning runs, the squid are literally present by the millions, and their presence attracts all types of predators which prey upon them they die, soon after they mate.

Occasionally, hordes of small, bright red crabs, known as pelagic red crabs invade the sand. Like the squid, these crabs normally inhabit the open sea, but at times they migrate to coastal waters. Their mating cycle is suspected to be the reason for the invasion, but that remains a point of speculation.

THE SARGASSO SEA

Not all areas within temperate seas are as prolific as kelp forests. The Sargasso Sea provides a classic example. It is a convergence of subtropical ocean currents, and the particular nature of the currents, makes it an area of shallow water with very poor circulation. The water is both warm and has high concentrations of salt.

Since almost no nutrient-rich water enters the Sargasso Sea, plankton production is very low by comparison, and it is often referred to as an aquatic desert. Yet some species manage to flourish.

The Sargasso Sea gets its name from the tremendous quantities of Sargassum weed that is produced there—approximately seven million tons in a 3,000-square-mile area. The floating rafts of Sargassum algae provide shelter and food for a specialized group of animals. Large numbers of eggs and larvae of open-ocean fishes become trapped in the Sargassum, providing a readily available food supply for raft residents, such as the well-known Sargassum fish or angler.

Consummate camouflage artists, Sargassum anglers have white-to-yellow bodies covered with dark patches, which allow them to blend in. They can also change their coloration as ambient light changes. Their bodies are covered with a number of flap-like projections, which make their outline look like that of Sargassum weed. The frilled front dorsal spine of the Sargassum angler dangles high in the water, serving as a lure for unsuspecting prey. As unwary victims move close to examine the dorsal spine, the angler quickly attacks.

Life in Coral Reef Communities

Coral reefs are often associated with paradisiacal tropical islands but, in fact, islands with coral reefs are generally rather small and desolate, with few trees and scrubby plants. Their true beauty lies below the surface, where massive coral reefs teem with a diversity of fascinating creatures.

INVERTEBRATES OF THE CORAL REEF COMMUNITY

Corals are actually living animals, and are closely related to sea anemones and jellyfish. These primitive organisms share many characteristics and are described in the phylum Cnidaria. Like all Cnidarians, corals capture their food with tentacles that are armed with stinging nematocysts. The individual animals, coral polyps, are attached to the bottom and sit in an external skeletal cup called a corallite. The skeletal cup is made from calcium carbonate, or limestone, and has been built by the coral itself.

The foundation of all coral reefs is built from the accumulated skeletal remains of once living corals, many of which existed thousands of years ago. Each living coral polyp secretes an external skeleton, made of calcium carbonate, which serves as the foundation for the reef. The living corals are found along the surface of the reef structure. As colonial corals grow, deposits of calcium carbonate increase as the reef structure expands.

In many shallow reefs, calcerous red algae live among the coral. The algae and other reef inhabitants secrete thin, yet vitally important, layers of limestone that greatly assist in the construction of the reef.

Hard, or true, corals are often considered to be the most significant invertebrates found in shallow, tropical waters. These are the building blocks of the magnificent limestone reefs that were created in the life processes of both once-living corals and other limestone-secreting, reef-dwelling organisms. All reef-building corals are colonial, though solitary corals occur in oceans throughout the world.

Coral reefs are limited to warm, clean, shallow tropical and subtropical waters with normal salinity, where the organisms that live in, on, and around the reefs can receive plenty of sunlight. True reef-building corals grow best where the average water temperature is between 73 and 77 degrees F (23 to 25° C). Most coral reefs are confined to waters that are shallower than 100 feet, although reefs have been documented below 200 feet.

True reef-building corals are partners in a symbiotic relationship (called mutualism) with a microscopic yellow algae, called zooxanthellae. Living in the surface tissues of the corals, zooxanthellae are unicellular algae which occur in high concentrations, and are responsible for most of the color we see in the coral. Though the relationship between zooxanthellae and corals is not completely understood, the corals provide the algae with a secure environment and plenty of nutrients from their own wastes, and in return, the corals receive oxygen as a byproduct of the algae's photosynthesis and avoid having to spend the costly energy of eliminating many cellular wastes.

In addition to the nutritional contribution of the zooxanthellae, corals are well-equipped to take advantage of other sources of food. In fact, some larger corals feed exclusively on small fish and larger forms of zooplankton (animal plankton). Species that have smaller polyps capture other organic particles that are as small as bacteria, tidbits of drifting fish slime, and other organic matter that has been dissolved in saltwater.

Coral reefs can generally be divided into three major groups, fringing reefs, barrier reefs, and atolls. Fringing reefs form borders near the shoreline of volcanic islands. Many of the reefs in Hawaii, for example, are fringing reefs. Barrier reefs, on the other hand, develop further offshore, near continental landmasses, and create a lagoon between themselves and the beach. The largest reef structure in the world is the Great Barrier Reef, which lies off the northeast coast of Australia. The Great Barrier Reef extends over 1,250 miles and, in places, is more than 150 miles wide. The second-largest barrier reef in the world is Turneffe Reef, which is located off the east coast of Belize in Caribbean waters. Atolls are ring-shaped coral reefs, with internal lagoons that occur above submerged volcanoes. Low islands which project above the sea's surface are often associated with atolls.

Reproduction in corals is not completely understood. As corals grow, they can either "bud off" (reproducing asexually) or they can produce planktonic larvae via sexual reproduction. Approximately 65 percent of corals are classified as broadcast spawners, with the males and females of the species first releasing chemicals that communicate to others that they are going to release sperm and eggs into the water. On Australia's Great Barrier Reef, more than 100 of the 340 species of coral found there spawn in this manner, and all spawn on the same spring night, once a year. However, in the Red Sea, none of the dominant species spawn at the same time as any other species.

Worldwide, there are more than 2,500 species of hard corals. The six major categories of shape are branching, brain, platy, encrusting, mushroom, and star.

Approximately 200 species of branching corals are usually found along the seaward edge of reefs, and are the most abundant of the reef-building corals in both the Atlantic and Indo-Pacific basins. The only two branching corals found in the Atlantic—elkhorn and staghorn—play prominent roles in Caribbean reef structures. Both are visually striking, their maze-like appearance looking much like miniature underwater forests, and are considered to be the major reef-building corals throughout the world.

Brain corals look like large round boulders, with a furrowed surface that resembles the surface of a human brain. The polyps reproduce by budding and new individuals are not completely separated from their parents. The interconnected polyps form long rows over the surface of the coral. Dominant genera in the Indo-Pacific include *Favia* and *Platygyra*, while the genus *Diploria* is the most common brain coral found in the Atlantic.

Despite their flowing appearance, platy corals are constructed in rigid sheets and are easily broken. The platy corals are made of thin sheets of calcium carbonate, supporting evenly distributed polyps.

Encrusting corals exist on thin sheets of calcium carbonate, draped over other blocks of coral. Encrusting corals often kill their hosts in the ongoing competition for space and food in reef communities. Fire corals, which often cover and kill sections of brain corals, are classic examples. Their cells can cause a fire-like sting followed by a painful rash.

Mushroom corals, found in tide pools and in deeper water along expanding edges of the reef, reproduce by budding, like the brain corals; new individuals, however, separate from their parents, creating the different surface appearance of mushrooms.

Star corals are large corals and look much like brain corals, but their individual polyps are separated rather than connected. The name "star coral" is derived from the star-shape of the individual polyps.

Even though soft corals are diverse and visually striking, they are not true reef-building corals. As a result, they are not considered to be as important in the existence of a healthy tropical reef community.

Soft corals include the wire corals, soft corals (order Alcyonacea), sea fans, and zoanthids.

Flowing Antipatharian corals, like many species of soft coral, are often referred to by casual observers as plants, due to their bush-like appearance. They are colonial corals, often called sea trees, wire corals, and black corals.

Both Alcyonacea soft corals and sea fans (which visually resemble large hand-held fans) are also commonly mistaken for colorful marine plants. Like other corals, these species are animals. Soft corals possess rows of tiny polyps, arranged on elongated flexible arms. These arms sway with current and water movement. Huge trees of cherry red, burgundy, yellow, and orange soft corals are favorite subjects for underwater photographers in the Indo-Pacific, where individual trees often reach heights of eight to 12 feet. Alcyonacea soft corals are rather rare in the Caribbean.

Colonial zoanthids are often found living on sponges and other invertebrates, as well as on the reef itself. These vivid yellow-to-orange corals, sometimes confused with anemones, can be distinguished by the rows of tentacles around their body, as opposed to the numerous tentacles of anemones. Another identifying characteristic is their size—usually quarter-sized or smaller. These corals lack a skeleton.

While it is important to realize that coral reefs themselves are living structures, the coral reefs around the world also serve as a places to live, a means of protection, and even a source of food for literally thousands of species of marine animals. Perhaps one of the most startling realizations for any beginning scuba diver or snorkeler is that almost every nook and cranny of every coral reef seems to be occupied or used by one type of animal or another. The reef's diversity and quantity of life is truly astonishing.

Appearing in an almost unending variety of shapes and colors, sponges are the simplest and most primitive of multicellular animals. Worldwide, there are in excess of 10,000 species of marine sponges. Their presence is especially notable on Caribbean reefs, where two- to 12-foot-high barrel sponges are found on the tops of many walls, while a variety of colorful rope and tube sponges stand out on many walls and drop-offs. Encrusting sponges add patches of brilliant color throughout the reef. Upon close examination, divers will often discover brittle stars, a variety of crabs, and some well-camouflaged fish taking up residence on sponges.

While many sponges are colonial, some are erect and lobed, and still others are encrusting. Because there is a wide variety of shapes, it is sometimes difficult for new divers to confidently identify sponges.

Sponges do not possess specialized tissues and organs. They feed by pumping water in through pores in their walls. Wastes are eliminated by pumping the waste-filled water out through a large opening called an osculum. By constantly circulating water through their systems, sponges serve the entire reef community by constantly filtering the water supply. In their larval stages sponges are free-swimming, but as adults they attach to the sea bottom.

The reef is also host to marine worms. Many marine worms are surprisingly attractive creatures. Multicolored specimens of feather dusters and Christmas tree worms form their own calcerous tubes, that they burrow into the live coral heads. Their delicate feather-like gills are often exposed up in the water column and are a favorite subject for underwater macro-photographers. They are sensitive to both light and current, and will retract their gills if disturbed.

Numerous echinoderms—sea stars (once called star fish), brittle stars, basket stars, feather stars, sea cucumbers, and sea urchins—play major roles in the reef ecology. While sea stars are not as prominent as they are in rocky reef communities, the crown-of-thorns is certainly noteworthy, as it feeds on coral polyps. Occasionally occurring in large numbers, it has at times caused well-publicized and rather extensive damage to expanses of the Great Barrier Reef.

Basket stars are often seen at night, perched atop sea fans. They feed at night by filtering plankton out of the water column and, when feeding, their unfurled arms give them a basket-like appearance. During the day, they retract their long arms, and most seek cover.

Brittle stars are quite common in coral reefs around the world. When overturned, almost every rock or large piece of rubble will expose a brittle star; but they quickly swim, crawl, and writhe their way back to cover. The thin arms of brittle stars radiate out from a generally rounded central disc. As with other echinoderms, the arms of brittle stars serve not only locomotive functions, but also assist in respiratory, excretory, and sensory roles.

Feather stars are ancient animals. Often called crinoids, they appear in a wide variety of colors, looking much like a group of feathers perched atop the reef, where they are able to capture food out of the water column.

Sea cucumbers are primarily scavengers, living adjacent to the reef in sandy areas, where they ingest bottom sediment in the search for food. Some species of sea cucumbers eject their own stomach in an effort to ward off predators.

Some sea urchins graze on algae that grow on the reef, while other species prey upon sea stars and other animals. Urchins protect their bodies with numerous long, sharp spines that inflict a painful wound to those who are careless about what they touch. While most urchins' spines are not long or sharp, almost all can inflict a painful jab that can cause considerable discomfort and infection.

Approximately one million species—close to two-thirds of all living species—are arthropods. They are well represented on coral reefs by a diversity of shrimps, crabs, barnacles, and lobsters.

Hundreds of species of shrimp live in coral reef communities. Many are spectacularly colored and have elaborate, ornate designs. Almost all are nocturnal, and night-divers often see the eyes of shrimp glowing in the dark, or giving off strong reflective beams when the eyes are struck by the beam from an underwater light. Like many nocturnal animals, they are usually quick to seek cover when exposed in light. Some species, such as the Caribbean shrimp, Pederson's cleaning shrimp, are the hosts of cleaning stations in reef communities.

Many crabs, including hermit, decorator, arrow, stone, and spider crabs, are vital members of coral communities. The size of these crustaceans can vary from that of a dime to several feet across. Decorator crabs plant anemones, pieces of sponges, and pieces of broken shells on their backs to help disguise themselves, while hermit crabs protect their vulnerable abdomens by seeking refuge in a "mobile home," made from the shell of a deceased snail.

Divers usually spot the colorful spiny lobster by sighting its antennae protruding from caves and crevices underneath coral heads. Both the spiny and slipper lobster will scavenge dead animals.

Among the most noteworthy gastropods are the giant clams found throughout much of the South Pacific, including the waters of the Great Barrier Reef. These bivalve mollusks can be more than three feet across, and have beautiful iridescent mantles that occur in shades of purple, blue, and green. (The color is supplied by the tiny zooxanthellae algae that live within the skin.) The Caribbean clam, called a fire or file shell, possesses a beautiful cherry-red mantle bordered by snow-white tentacles and, like the flamingo tongue cowrie, is considered to be one of the Caribbean's prettiest mollusks. Many species of nudibranchs, especially several varieties of the brilliant red Spanish dancer, are equally spectacular.

Octopi are among the cleverest of reef creatures. They are major predators of other mollusks and small fish, and are a favorite food of moray eels. Their close relatives, the squid, serve as a vital food source for a great many reef fish.

VERTEBRATES OF THE CORAL REEF COMMUNITY

Although reptiles, such as sea snakes and turtles, are present in many coral reef communities, it is the many species of fish that are the most prominent vertebrates. Worldwide, there are approximately 18,850 species of fish, almost half of the 42,000 vertebrates known to science. Coral reefs provide a protective cover, a source of food, and a place to hunt for food for many species of fish. Several genera (the plural of genus) are found in all major coral reef communities. Included in this group are the moray eels, sharks, rays, and skates; butterfly fish, squirrel fish, porcupine fish, groupers, triggerfish; and a variety of gobies, wrasse, surgeonfish, and seahorses.

Morays are fish, but they lack the gill covers present in most bony fish, and must continuously open and close their mouths to pump oxygenated water over their gills. In the act of breathing the eels expose their teeth.

Morays are one of the major predators in reef communities, feeding on fish, crustaceans, and mollusks—especially octopi. Other major predators include the great barracuda and a variety of reef sharks.

Barracuda have the rather annoying habit of hovering around swimmers and divers. They rarely attack people, but if they do, their long canine-like teeth can inflict serious wounds. Among the fastest of swimmers, barracudas prey upon a variety of smaller reef fish.

Prominent species of tropical reef sharks include bull sharks, lemon sharks, silky sharks, black tips, nurse sharks, tiger sharks, grey reef sharks, some hammerheads, silver tips, whitetip reef sharks, the banded catsharks, and and the wobbegongs or carpet sharks.

Some of the more active species include the lemon, bull, tiger, grey reef, silver tip, and the hammerheads. These sharks travel great distances each day and most undertake some seasonal migration following changes in water temperature. As a rule, they tend to move closer toward the warmer waters of the equator during winter.

The bottom-dwellers spend most of their time simply resting on the ocean floor, moving only to seek food. Many of them, like wobbegongs, hardly move at all. Well-camouflaged, they wait for food to come to them before quickly lunging at their prey. But there are notable exceptions: the nurse, zebra, and the tawny nurse shark are larger than many other bottom-dwelling species and will cover a much greater area.

Most reef sharks are moderately sized, typically attaining a length of between three and 10 feet. Their size makes them large reef predators, while still being small enough to maneuver in the tight quarters of a reef. Tropical reef sharks do not usually gather in schools—with a notable exception being the scalloped hammerheads, which sometime congregate by the hundreds. However, while the reef sharks do not typically congregate in tight schools, they do tend to congregate in given areas; if you see a grey reef shark on any given dive, you have an excellent chance of seeing several more.

Grey reef sharks, common throughout the South Pacific, are well known for an exaggerated pre-attack display which sometime occurs. In this display, the grey reef sharks arch their backs, tuck their pectoral fins, and swim in a herky-jerky manner before attacking. Because of the notoriety these displays have received, many people believe all sharks posture in this manner before attacking their prey. This misconception is only one of many. Even grey reef sharks do not always display.

Most reef sharks are capable of quick bursts of speed that enable them to capture small fish before those fish can escape into the safe confines of the reef. Tropical reef sharks prefer to feed on a wide variety of fish, crustaceans, and mollusks.

The sand patches and plains which surround the coral reefs are also inhabited by a variety of fish species, including flounder. Flounder are easy to overlook because they are experts at blending in with the sea floor. Specialized cells in their skin enable these flatfish to rapidly change their color and pattern to blend in with their surroundings.

Aside from flounder, perhaps the most notable bottom-dweller is the sting ray. Stingrays feed on a variety of fish, crustaceans, and mollusks. The threat of stepping on a sting ray—animals that are well-equipped to defend themselves with one or more barbs on their tail—poses a great risk to divers and swimmers. Sting rays like to rest on sandy bottoms between patches of reef, often covering themselves with sand. If stepped on, rays will defend themselves by stinging or barbing. Before walking across sand patches, wise swimmers and divers pound and shuffle their feet, so the rays will be forewarned of their presence and leave.

Not all rays possess barbed stingers. Some rays, generally called electric rays, have special organs that produce electricity, used to stun their prey and ward off predators. While most rays are excellent swimmers, electric rays tend to be more sluggish.

Still other fish, like the lionfish and turkeyfish, protect themselves with poisonous dorsal spines. These species are brilliantly colored and tend to stand out against a reef background. Relatively poor swimmers, lion- and turkeyfish protect themselves by jabbing potential predators with their large dorsal spines. Trumpetfish, on the other hand, use camouflage to mimic the surrounding coral.

Slow-swimming porcupine fish, often called puffers or blowfish, utilize a rather unique adaptation to protect themselves. When threatened, they swallow water until their stomachs are completely distended. This action erects numerous sharp spines all over their bodies, making them rather uninviting targets.

Many species of fishes such as snapper, grunts, jacks, and surgeonfish (commonly called tang) school or group in large numbers. Scientists believe that fish school for a variety of reasons that deal with the concept of survival of the species. A school of small fish can appear to be one big shape, large enough to ward off potential predators. Schooling also confuses predators: the predator takes time to pick out a single target, all the fish have time to escape. One other theory maintains that schooling enables many small fish to outproduce what larger predators can consume.

Jewfish, which can weigh more than 700 pounds, and groupers are among the largest predators in tropical reef communities. Most of these species are solitary, and are often seen near the bottom, sitting in caves or protective openings.

Butterfly fish are among the most ornately decorated of all tropical reef fish. They are diurnal foragers, feeding on benthic worms and shrimp, as well as on the coral itself—especially the tentacles of zoanthid corals. Butterfly fishes' similar markings on the head and tail are thought to increase their chances of survival, as predators might misjudge the direction that the butterfly fish will move.

Cleaning symbiosis is a form of mutualism that is quite common in coral reef communities. The partner known as the cleaner—some shrimp and several types of fish, including wrasse, butterfly fish, gobies, and juvenile angelfish—pick parasites, dead tissue, and bacteria off the skin of the host fish. At times, species of grouper, tang, coneys, hinds, and other fish will line up at cleaning stations waiting to be cleaned.

Gobies comprise the single largest family of tropical reef fish. Most are small benthic fish, found on coral, in the rubble zone, or in sand. Waiting to dart out at prey, gobies usually lie on their outstretched ventral fins. While some species are quite colorful, many associate with other animals such as tube sponges, anemones, and urchins, and these species are well-camouflaged to match their backgrounds. Several varieties of neon gobies are active cleaners; these fish are brightly colored in an effort to attract host fish to their cleaning stations. The family of wrasses are abundant members of the coral reef community. These small, cigar-shaped predators will eat almost any small organism. Most species are diurnal, with some hogfish being exceptions. While some are particularly active at cleaning stations, others tend to follow schools of goatfish, rays, and other predators, hoping to pick up left-overs.

There are two types of males: primary males which live their entire lives as males, and secondary males which begin life as females. If the dominant or "supermale" within a given population dies, the largest and most dominant male or female will become the dominant male within only a few days.

Numerous species of parrotfish feed on algae in small groups, each dominated by a single male. They have large, heavy teeth, fused together to form a beak-like jaw. Divers can hear the crunching sound made by their grinding away on the reef as they feed. Parrotfish in the genera *Scarus* and *Cryptotomus* sleep in self-made mucus cocoons, which they create in order to mask their smell. The cocoon helps parrotfish avoid moray eels and other predators, who rely heavily on their olfactory senses to locate prey.

High up in the water column, divers find fishes as varied as needlefish and pompano. Needlefishes are cigar-shaped fish that tend to gather in small schools just below the surface, where their silver coloration helps them blend in with the water. Attracted by the lights from anchoring boats, needlefish often "jump" out of the water.

Pompano are described in the Family Carangidae, which also contains jacks and scads. Found in all tropical seas, pompano prefer to school. The juveniles possess long, trailing filaments that are often much longer than the rest of the body. They tend to remain inshore, often following rafts of debris or seaweed, while adults tend to live in deeper waters.

A variety of vividly colored species of clownfish are feature attractions on many Indo-Pacific reefs. Clownfish often share a symbiotic relationship with the anemones *Stoichactis* and *Actinia.* The clownfish coat themselves with protective mucus, which allows them to nestle amongst the stinging tentacles of the anemone without being harmed. The wriggling antics of the brightly colored clowns are probably intended to lure other fishes to the stinging tentacles of the only slightly mobile anemones. Since the anemone is quick to sting other fishes that come within touching distance of their tentacles, both the clownfish and the anemone end up with a meal.

There are 60 species of marine snakes. Many are found in the tropical reefs of the Indo-Pacific region. All species are bottom-feeders, and none are known to actively pursue swimming prey.

They are armed with deadly forms of neurotoxins that quickly incapacitate their prey—usually small fish. The bite from some species will easily kill a person, but attacks on swimmers and divers are extremely rare. Throughout the South Pacific, net fishermen report fatalities from accidents occurring when fishermen try to disentangle sea snakes from their nets. Though most sea snakes have small mouths, they are capable of opening them extremely wide and can easily impale their fangs on targets of many sizes. During their mating seasons, some species swarm together in large balls. Some experts maintain that the snakes do show some aggression toward divers during that time.

Sea turtles are commonly encountered on many tropical reefs. Leatherback turtles are the largest of all, weighing up to 1,600 pounds. By comparison, a full-grown loggerhead, which is considered a large turtle, attains a weight of only 1,000 pounds. Despite their size, these turtles are excellent swimmers and some species have been clocked at over 35 miles per hour.

Perhaps turtles are best-known for their nesting habits. All lay eggs in holes, dug in sandy beaches on tropical and sub-tropical coasts. In fact, green turtles nest on the exact beaches where they were hatched. Exactly how green turtles find these small isolated beaches, after long journeys at sea, remains a mystery to science.

Life in the Open Sea

Open ocean animals range from the tiniest forms of phytoplankton (plant plankton) and zooplankton (animal plankton)—which occupy the lowest levels of oceanic food webs—to the largest apex predators, like shark, whales, and fishes such as tuna, marlin, and swordfish. While these apex predators occupy the top rungs of their respective food chains, their ability to exist is predicated on the presence of phytoplankton and zooplankton, which form their food chain's foundation.

The simple plants, known as diatoms and dinoflagellates, are the most abundant forms of phytoplankton and play important roles in every major oceanic food chain. The term "zooplankton" describes a range of animals that vary from permanent open-ocean organisms, such as small crustaceans, to the larvae of what will later develop into benthic (or bottom-dwelling) creatures. The California spiny lobster is a classic case of an animal that is planktonic in its larval stage, and a benthic reef-dweller as an adult.

The presence of plankton attracts larger animals like sardines, herring, and anchovies. In some food chains, the small pelagic fishes are preyed upon by mackerel and smelt, who are in turn sought after by yellowtail, barracuda, bonito, and tuna. But the food chain does not stop here; middle predators are hunted by a variety of sharks, dolphins, and other marine mammals.

OPEN-OCEAN INVERTEBRATES

In addition to planktonic organisms, other invertebrates, such as comb jellies and jellyfish can also appear in enormous concentrations. Worldwide, there are approximately 200 species; all are Cnidarians and capture their prey through the stinging cells in their tentacles. In some species, the tentacles trail out for as long as 60 feet behind the bell. They serve as a lure, attracting fishes who unsuspectingly investigate or bump into them.

One species of jellyfish that is occasionally seen in dense concentrations in the open ocean off the coast of California is *Velella lata*, commonly called "by-the-wind-sailors." The clear bell of these jellyfish attains a diameter of close to four inches. The bell is surrounded by a blue to purple border. This species is characterized by the small membrane called a "sail" which sits atop the bell.

Another especially attractive species found off the coast of western North America is the California purple striped jellyfish. It can be distinguished by its white to milky-white bell with regularly spaced longitudinal purple stripes. The intensity of the purple varies from individual to individual. As a rule, the more vivid the purple, the more stunning the specimen.

A variety of translucent moon jellies are common in tropical waters while several species of disk jellies are common in temperate and polar seas.

All jellyfish are relatively primitive, having only a simple system of nerve nets. Lacking both a brain and centrally controlled muscles, they are relatively poor swimmers, and are at the mercy of the currents. The nerve nets in the bell control the rhythmic pulsations used in swimming.

The sea wasps (also known as box jellies) and the Portuguese man-of-war deserve special mention. Stings from these species contain some of the most powerful marine toxins and can prove fatal to humans. Sea wasps usually come up from the depths to surface waters at night. They are often attracted to the lights of anchored boats.

The float or bell of a Portuguese man-of-war is usually blue or purple and is only a foot or so in diameter. But beware! The dangerous stinging tentacles can trail as far as 20 yards behind the bell. A commensal fish, the man-of-war mackerel, lives among the tentacles without being stung. This small fish attracts other fishes to the man-of-war and receives food and protection in return.

A variety of comb jellies are found in the open sea, drifting with the currents. Upon first glance, comb jellies are easily mistaken for jellyfish, but with only a little effort, it is easy to distinguish comb jellies from jellyfish. Comb jellies are invertebrates described in the phylum Ctenophora. They take on a variety of shapes other the normal bell shape of jellyfish. The single most important distinguishing characteristic is that comb jellies have eight ciliated "combs," which look like lines covered by tiny hairs. The rows of cilia allow for independent locomotion in comb jellies, but they remain poor swimmers and their location is usually dictated by current flow. Some forms are bioluminescent, creating their own light.

OPEN-OCEAN VERTEBRATES

Sea turtles, huge manta rays, numerous species of sharks; fast-swimming bony fishes such as mackerel, bonito, tuna, swordfish, and marlin, and a host of dolphins and whales roam the surface waters of the open ocean. However, the most surprising vertebrates are called salp.

Salp occur in a variety of shapes and sizes, but most can be roughly described as gelatinous masses. Most are translucent, and some salp are linked together in long chains exceeding 40 feet in length. These chains look somewhat like a string of large clear beads. Even though salp lack a distinct skull, they are primitive vertebrates, and in their larval stages, they have a notocord, which is analogous to a very primitive spinal column.

Several species of rays are often seen in open-sea settings, but none are more spectacular than the Pacific manta. Observed throughout the Pacific, mantas are migratory creatures. They lack the stinger or barb present in bottom-dwelling rays.

Like all cartilaginous fishes, mantas lack a swim bladder; they must keep swimming to avoid sinking. Manta rays do not have "true" wings, but do possess a pair of very large pectoral fins which are commonly called wings. The fins can be manipulated independently and provide considerable thrust and maneuverability. These rays are often spotted by boaters in calm waters as the tips of their large pectorals stand above the surface.

Mantas have horn-like appendages on the front of their heads, called cephalic lobes, that aid in funnelling plankton into the ray's mouth during feeding. Manta rays feed primarily upon plankton and small fish, and are often seen doing backward rolls underwater as they use their cephalic lobes to shovel food into their cavernous mouths.

Other open-sea cartilaginous fishes include a variety of sharks. The world's largest shark, the basking shark, is documented to attain a length of 50 feet. It does not, however, receive much notoriety, probably because it is a filter feeder.

Certainly, oceanic whitetips are among the most dramatic of the open sea sharks found in the tropical waters of the Indo-Pacific. These magnificent creatures are often accompanied by a school of pilot fish. Blue sharks, and shortfin mako sharks are the most commonly seen open-sea sharks in temperate waters. So named for their iridescent blue coloration, blue sharks are considered by many to be among the prettiest of sharks. They prey upon small schooling fishes and squid.

Shortfin makos are in the same family of sharks as great whites, and are among the most dramatic-looking species. They are very stocky and rather herky-jerky in their swimming movement, as opposed to blue sharks; and they have a large, reinforced, symmetrically shaped tail-fin, which provides plenty of speed.

Several species of thresher sharks are also very numerous open-ocean sharks, but most are believed to be primarily nocturnal species and are only rarely seen by divers.

There are 43 species of flying fishes. The largest species is the California flying fish, while the Atlantic flying fish is the most common species on both sides of the Atlantic. These fish acquired their names from their rather unique ability to leave the water—in what looks like flight—in an effort to escape predation from a variety of fish and dolphins. The glides of some species can last for up to 13 seconds and easily cover 150 yards at speeds up to 35 miles per hour.

When flying fish leave the water, they rapidly beat the lower lobe of their tail back and forth to gain speed. Boats often scare these fish into "flight."

Several species of mackerel play vital roles in open-ocean food chains. Mackerel are heavily preyed upon by porpoises, sea lions, yellowtail, marlin, and sharks. In turn, the Pacific, the bullet, and the skipjack mackerel feed upon small fishes, planktonic crustaceans, and juvenile squid. Most are medium-sized fish, weighing from several ounces to less than five pounds, but skipjack can be as long as 40 inches and weigh as much as 35 pounds.

Bonito are common in all tropical and temperate seas. Members of the tuna family, bonito are fast swimmers. They are often seen in extremely dense schools numbering into the tens of thousands. Bonito are easily excited, as are many tuna, and often swirl rapidly around divers, tightening the circle as their excitement increases. They are medium-sized fish in the 15- to 40-inch range; most are dark blue above, with silverish undersides.

Yellowtail (Seriola) are a schooling fish, popular among many game fishermen. Yellows, as they are often called, are found in a variety of habitats—close to shore, at off shore islands, over off shore banks, and drifting under open ocean kelp paddies. They are occasionally seen rubbing themselves against the skin of large sharks, especially blues, which scientists suspect is an effort to rid themselves of parasites. Some mackerel demonstrate a similar behavior.

One of the most unusual open-ocean fish is the ocean sunfish, or Mola mola. They are disc-shaped fish that look somewhat like an overgrown frisbee with fins. Molas are often mistaken for sharks, as their long pectoral fins often stick up past the surface. A large ocean sunfish can easily exceed 13 feet in length and weigh over 3,000 pounds. Ocean sunfish are commonly attracted to anything that can be described as an "event" in the ocean, such as a boat, a piece of driftwood, or a floating kelp paddy.

Tuna—and their close relatives the swordfish, sailfish, and marlin—are among the sea's most beautiful creatures. They are delicately colored, have wonderfully streamlined bodies, and are considered to be biologically advanced, having evolved to an unsurpassed level of hydrodynamic refinement. Tuna and billfish (swordfish, sailfish, and marlin) are some of the fastest swimmers in the sea.

Unlike all other fish, tuna and billfish are warm-blooded. In order to maintain their higher body-temperature in cool waters, these fish must consume incredible quantities of food. In fact, some species eat up to 10 percent of their body weight everyday!

In all species of tuna, a spawning female releases approximately 100,000 eggs for every kilogram (2.2 pounds) of body weight! That means a 145-pound (medium-sized) tuna will release more than 6.5 million eggs in one spawning.

Billfish are known for their long sword-like beaks which extend out from their upper jaw, which are believed to be used to stun the small fish that are among their prey. Compared to tuna, less is known about this highly migratory fish.

Black marlin are probably the largest fish of all bony fishes, and large specimens are documented to weigh in excess of 2,900 pounds.

The open sea appears to be a uniform setting, but that is not the case. The bottom terrain varies greatly, as do surface conditions. With these factors, the distribution of whales and dolphins also varies. In many areas, the open sea is almost devoid of life, while in others, the density of life is staggering. As a general rule, these open-ocean deserts and meccas are a function of currents and water conditions, which also impact the presence or absence of plankton.

Extensive studies of the waters of the Eastern Pacific have demonstrated that, in waters where most tuna fishing occurs, and where water temperature is fairly constant, spinner and spotter dolphins dominate. However, where water temperatures fluctuate, the most common species are striped dolphins and common dolphins.

In the waters off of the coast of southern California, in an area known as the California Bight, the distribution of both pilot whales and common dolphins has been linked to sea-floor topography, even though the sea floor is hundreds of feet beneath the surface. Pilot whales prefer to feed on squid that gather around undersea mountains; as a result, pilot whales are far more likely to be found in areas where the sea floor is mountainous. Common dolphins tend to be found more often over flat bottoms, even though the bottom can be very deep. At times common dolphins gather by the tens of thousands.

Some dolphins and whales that seem to prefer to inhabit the open sea include the northern bottlenose whale (found in the cool temperate and polar waters of the North Atlantic), Baird's beaked whale, Pacific white-sided dolphins, and Risso's dolphin.

Baleen whales undertake some of the longest migrations known to science. Their migrations are influenced by factors such as the abundance and distribution of food, and the preferred conditions in sites used for calving and mating. Of the large pelagic toothed whales, only the migration of the sperm whale is well understood. Sperm whales often form large "rafts" or pods, and members of these rafts can be seen gathered tightly together on the surface out in the open sea.

While the vast majority of large, active swimming, marine organisms live their lives within 600 feet of the surface, towards the bottom of and below the photic zone, where very little sunlight penetrates into the darkness, exist other forms of life. This depth, below 600 feet to approximately 3,000 feet, is referred to as the mesopelagic zone. In some respects, conditions in the mesopelagic zone offer considerable advantages over conditions in the photic zone. For example, predators find it more difficult to locate prey in the low-light conditions.

Certainly, from the prey's perspective, low light is a huge advantage. Lower water temperatures tend to reduce the metabolic rates of mesopelagic fishes so they need less food and less oxygen to survive. There is constant "rain" of organic particles for food, as the increased density of cold water slows the rate of descent of food particles, making them available for longer than it would be in near-surface waters.

At times, large numbers of mesopelagic creatures migrate vertically toward surface waters to feed. In temperate and tropical seas, just after sunset, many organisms rise vertically through the water column into surface waters to feed and, as a rule, they descend again before daybreak. In productive polar seas, the pattern breaks down and just the opposite is true. Related organisms spend the summer high up in the photic zone and the winter in deeper waters.

Most fishes of the mesopelagic zone have small bodies (less mass to support), large mouths to help capture prey, and a variety of lures to attract prey. Some of these lures are body appendages, looking like tidbits of food. Species with these types of frilled appendages are commonly called anglerfish.

Some fishes utilize light cells, called photophores, to create bioluminescent light, both to attract prey and also as a form of communication with members of their own species. Still others discharge luminescent secretions into the water, or have light-producing bacteria in their own body tissues, to attract unsuspecting prey.

The scarcity of food in the deep sea also means that the population of any given species is likely to be low, and the chance for finding a mate is reduced. One male anglerfish—who is the smaller of the species—permanently attaches himself to a female her via interconnected bloodstreams. The function of the parasitic male is to provide sperm, making him little more than a reproductive organ on the female.

Mesopelagic fishes include a variety of anglerfish, the "great swallower," widemouths, the "gulper," lanternfishes, and hatchetfish. Another is the legendary giant squid. While little is known about the biology of giant squid, their existence is not a matter of speculation. These have been documented to attain a size of 60 feet and a weight of 1,000 pounds. They can have eyes the size of volleyballs and tentacles that are 30 feet long.

In recent years, a series of fascinating discoveries have been made, through the use of submarines, at the edges of moving tectonic plates on the sea floor. Scientists have found a variety of creatures that exist without oxygen (thought necessary to support all life forms on earth) by means of a life process known as chemosynthesis. Many scientists believe this discovery to be proof that life might be present on other planets where there is no oxygen.

Life in the Polar Seas

Despite harsh living conditions found in the polar regions, many species are able to flourish. Aided by high winds, strong currents, and constant upwellings, the mineral-rich waters of the Arctic and Antarctic continually produce rich concentrations of phytoplankton. During the extended daylight hours of the polar summer, the constant sunlight intensifies the natural production of phytoplankton and the phytoplankton's density in surface waters increases dramatically. The presence of these massive quantities of phytoplankton enables the tiny invertebrates and fish larvae known as zooplankton to flourish. Zooplankton feed upon phytoplankton, and are quick to multiply when the amount of food increases.

Both the phytoplankton and zooplankton are heavily preyed upon by numerous species. Many of the larger animals that feed upon both phytoplankton and zooplankton have evolved specially modified mouths, allowing them to filter large amounts of plankton from the water column. Most of the oceans largest animals, including blue, humpback, sei, bowhead, and fin whales are filter feeders.

Many smaller species of crustaceans, and some fish larvae, also possess specially adapted filter-feeding mechanisms, such as hair-like filaments in their mouths, which they use to help scoop up and trap plankton.

Large schools of fish, like herring, also congregate near the dense concentrations of plankton and are preyed upon by a variety of birds, seals—hooded, ringed or jar, banded, harp or Greenland, and others—as well as toothed whales, such as killer whales, narwhals, beluga whales, and several species of dolphins. In the Antarctic, sea elephants, leopard, Weddell's, crabeater, and Ross seals enter the fray.

Even polar bears, primarily considered to be land animals, are part of the Arctic Ocean food web. Apex predators, polar bears are more carnivorous than most bears, and are indisputably the masters of the Arctic ice. Large males attain a length of just over 10 feet and, at that length, weigh about 2,500 pounds. Even when on all fours, a large polar bear stands almost five feet high.

Despite their massive size, these bears are capable of surprisingly fast and agile movement on ice. Superb swimmers and tireless travelers, polar bears cover great distances in their quest for food. Polar bears only rarely seek out land, preferring to live on Arctic ice floes or to swim across large expanses of sea.

Of all their prey, it is believed that polar bears prefer ringed or jar seals. In winter, when the surface of the sea is frozen over, polar bears wait patiently by holes in the ice that the seals use for breathing. When a seal appears, the polar bear breaks the seal's back with a strong blow from its paw, then drags its victim from the water. Polar bears are versatile and willingly prey upon small mammals, bird eggs, algae, and carrion when food is scarce.

PINNIPEDS OF THE POLAR SEAS

Seals and sea lions share many common physiological characteristics, such as having heavy layers of fat underneath a thick hide—an adaptation which protects them against the cold. Both seals and sea lions possess modified fore- and hind-flippers which assist in maneuvering both on land and in water. But while laymen often use the terms seals and sea lions interchangeably, biologically speaking, there are significant differences between the sea lions and true seals. First, sea lions possess small external ears which seals lack. (It is, however, considered correct to call sea lions "earred seals.") Secondly, the fore-flippers of sea lions are comparatively large and are used as the chief means of propulsion in water. Sea lions use their rear-flippers as a rudder, while seals use their hind-flippers for propulsion. Because they can turn their rear-flippers forward, sea lions demonstrate superior maneuverability on land. Finally, sea lions possess a harsh coat, while the more handsome coat of true seals consists of a dense, soft undercoat, protected by guard hairs. The coats of most sea lions do not offer as much insulation as those of true seals and, as a result, most sea lions are to be found in sub-polar rather than polar seas.

Both seals and sea lions are highly social animals, preferring to gather in large herds at many times during the course of a year. Northern sea lions, the most notable species of sea lion found within the Arctic Circle, sometimes gather in huge colonies which number in excess of a million animals. As a rule, sea lion and seal pups, as well as non-breeding females, are much more gregarious than mature males and breeding females.

In the case of Northern sea lions, the males travel north just prior to the onset of their spring mating season. The males claim and ferociously protect a territory, in which they are determined to be the only breeding male, and can have up to 50 females in their harems. Approximately one month later, the females and young arrive. The juveniles form a separate group. Shortly after their arrival, the females give birth and, not too long after, they are able to breed again. In the fall, when the pups are capable of making a migration, the herds head south, toward the warmer waters of Japan and California.

Several species of seals and sea lions can be found in Arctic and subarctic regions, such as the harbour or common, ringed, harp or Greenland, banded, bearded seal, hooded, and the Alaskan fur seal. Alaskan fur seals, though small when compared to many other seals, have a thick soft fur which has been highly valued by man.

Walruses are easily the largest pinnipeds found in Arctic waters. These behemoths reach a length of almost 13 feet and at that length weigh close to 3,000 pounds. In addition to their massive size, walruses are easy to identify by their small heads and large tusks, present in both males and females. The males, whose tusks can be up to three feet long, use them to fight other males for females during breeding season. Both sexes use their tusks to protect ward off potential predators and to plough the sea floor as they search for a variety of worms, fish, and bivalve mollusks. The tusks are also used to assist in climbing and when walking over ice.

Walruses live exclusively near the coasts where they find their food. During winter, the animals migrate south with the floating ice, and in the summer they return to northern areas. Excellent swimmers, walruses can achieve speeds of close to 15 miles per hour. Walruses breed only once every two years. The young are preyed upon by killer whales and polar bears.

The majority of Antarctic seals, such as Weddell's seals, never haul out onto dry land, but live instead on ice floes, or on the frozen ice along the coast. Weddell's seals have dark grey fur on their backs, with a lighter shade on their chests and abdomens. These seals grow to about 10 feet long and spend a lot of summer hours basking in the warm sunlight as they rest on ice floes. In the winter, Weddell's seals take refuge below the ice and breathe through specially made holes.

Other common Antarctic species are crabeater and leopard seals. The crabeater seal has silvery fur and feeds exclusively on a variety of zooplankton, which it filters through specially adapted teeth. A species found only in the Antarctic, leopard seals are very aggressive predators and are the major enemy of penguins. Leopard seals will readily feed on shrimp and some mollusks, but they demonstrate a distinct preference for penguins which they attack both on ice and in water.

The sea elephant is found only in the southern hemisphere and breeds only on subantarctic islands. Its related species, the elephant seal, lives in the northern Pacific. Though they are the largest of all seals—with full-grown adult males measuring more than 20 feet and weighing in excess of four tons, they are are preyed upon by killer whales and leopard seals.

With the noted exception of leopard seals, most seals and sea lions feed on a variety of fish, crustaceans and mollusks—especially cuttlefish and squid; and are hunted by sperm whales, killer whales, polar bears, and, in some cases, man.

WHALES OF THE POLAR SEAS

Many species of both toothed and baleen whales (animals described in the order Cetacea) spend either all or part of their lives in the waters of the Arctic and Antarctic. Polar waters are rich in shoals of plankton, and filter-feeding whales. Known as baleen whales, they feed by opening their mouths as wide as they can, while swimming through concentrations of zooplankton commonly called krill. (True krill, *Euphausia superba*, exist only in Antarctic waters, but other krill-like crustaceans do inhabit the waters of all oceans. The long fibers of baleen found in the mouths of filter-feeding whales look somewhat like the bristles of an enormous scrub brush, and are used to trap food particles.

Many baleen whales spend the summers feeding in polar and sub-polar seas before beginning a migration toward temperate and tropical water as winter approaches. Humpback whales are a perfect case in point. Humpbacks are known in all oceans, up to the edges of polar ice packs, where many adults spend the summer months. They are, however, highly migratory; the same adults spend their summer months in tropical seas. Well known for their famous songs (believed to be used to communicate with other whales over long distances), humpbacks are seen both in open ocean and in coastal waters during different segments of their migrations.

Baleen whales are sometimes referred to as the "great whales," due to the huge sizes attained by blue whales, fin whales, and humpbacks. Blue whales commonly attain sizes of 100 feet and 100 tons, greatly exceeding the length of even the largest known dinosaurs. When full-grown, the smaller fin whale commonly reaches a length of 60 feet; the humpback attains a maximum size of about 57 feet and 50 tons.

Valuable insight into life in the sea can be gained by the realization that these incredible sizes are attained by animals that are filter feeders. There is far more plankton—in terms of biomass—to support these huge filter feeders than there are fishes or other food sources, which are preyed upon by the generally smaller toothed whales. Even the largest sharks—the whale shark and basking shark—are filter feeders. By comparison, the largest documented specimen of the largest species of carnivorous shark, the great white, was 21 feet long and weighed a mere 7,000 pounds.

Toothed whales are also well represented in polar waters. These include sperm, killer, and pilot whales; bottle-nosed, white-sided, and common dolphins. Other toothed whales, the white or beluga whale, and the narwhal, are found only in Arctic seas. Toothed whales tend to prefer to prey upon squid, cuttlefish, a variety of species of small schooling fish; in the case of sperm and killer whales, marine mammals, such as seals, sea lions, and other whales, are at risk.

As a group, the toothed whales demonstrate some remarkable adaptations. Toothed whales orient themselves and seek their prey by echolocating, emitting a series of up to 800 clicks per second and listening for the reflected echoes. Echolocating whales and dolphins can gauge the distance and speed of prey, as well as distinguish one object from the next, by noting the difference in the reflected sound caused by objects with different densities.

Sperm whales have an amazing ability to make deep dives in the pursuit of prey. They are known to be able to remain submerged for as long as 75 minutes, diving as deep as 3,250 feet. Like other marine mammals, sperm whales use a number of specialized adaptations to avoid the "bends," a malady suffered by the divers when they make too rapid an ascent to safely "outgas" the increased nitrogen that has been absorbed by their bodies. These whales are able to slow their heart beat when they dive, reducing the amount of nitrogen absorbed, and they also reduce circulation to some peripheral body parts.

Killer whales, often called orcas, are also found in both Arctic and Antarctic waters. It is a truly unforgettable sight to see the two-meter-tall dorsal fin on the back of a male killer whale break the surface as he swims by, often at speeds up to 30 miles per hour. Killer whales often work together when hunting both fish and other marine mammals. In recent years, it has been discovered that the pods of whales are controlled by dominant female, despite the larger size attained by males.

The beautiful white beluga whales, found in Arctic seas, are considered by many to be one of the prettiest species of cetaceans. Reaching a maximum length of about 16 feet, belugas prey upon a wide variety of fishes, especially salmon, crustaceans, and octopi. During the winter months, belugas tend to form small groups; during summer, they gather in large herds in many bays. These whales are known to swim hundreds of miles up major rivers.

The narwhal, sometimes called the unicorn whale, is a member of the same family of whales as the beluga. The species is notable for its famous spiral tusk, a highly developed tooth possessed by the males. Narwhals reach a length of about 15 feet (excluding the tusk); the tusk can extend another nine feet. The males use the tusk in fights for dominance.

Narwhals generally form pods of three to 20 whales, but can gather together in large aggregations of up to 2,000 animals, as they migrate during the change of seasons. Superb divers, these whales commonly reach depths in excess of 1,000 feet in the pursuit of food. While they are hunted by polar bears and killer whales, it is exploitation by man that poses the greatest threat to the species' survival. Their meat is eaten by Arctic peoples and the tusks are carved for ivory and for souvenirs.

BIRDS OF THE POLAR REGIONS

Many species of birds play important roles in the biological cycles of both the Arctic and Antarctic. During the warmer months of the year, the coasts of the Arctic are colonized by hundreds of thousands of sea birds, such as shags, gannets, guillemots, razorbills, puffins and other members of the auk family, gulls, and many other species. These birds scour the sea for food. Many of the larger species, like shags and gannets, are superb divers, often plummeting to depths of more than 300 feet to search for crustaceans, and mollusks. Gannets, however, appear to experience some difficulty when taking off from both flat ground and the surface of the sea. They are forced to run and flap—much like ducks and geese—before gaining enough lift to achieve flight. For these reasons, they much prefer to launch from cliffs. Most smaller species skim the surface for their food.

Some birds, like gannets and auks, build simple nests near the coast of small islands. The nests are built in very close proximity to one another, only a few feet apart, but the adults are capable of locating their nests immediately, upon returning from their food-gathering missions. Adults vigorously defend their nests against intruders.

Guillemots or murres, on the other hand, do not build nests—they simply deposit their eggs on the narrow ledges of small cliffs. Guillemot eggs are oblong rather than round; if bumped, the eggs will roll around in a small circle, rather than off the edge of a cliff. Guillemot eggs are incubated by both parents.

Many other species of birds are attracted to the Arctic and subarctic regions during summer by both the abundance of food and the safety provided by relative isolation. Albatrosses, petrels, and fulmars are some of the species of birds which spend their entire non-breeding lives either flying over or resting on the surface of the sea, and migrate to the Arctic and subarctic to breed. Waders like curlews, plovers, and sandpipers can be found throughout estuaries and along rivers, as they use their long, narrow beaks to dig small invertebrates out of the mud. A variety of ducks, geese, and shearwaters, as well as bald eagles and sea eagles (osprey), also inhabit Arctic regions.

The overwhelming majority of the 40 species of birds that nest in the Antarctic are seabirds. While this amount in an area the size of Antarctica represents a distinct lack of variety, paucity is balanced by sheer numbers.

Most of the seabirds nest near coastal edges, but there are exceptions. The snow petrels nest on mountain peaks at altitudes up to 6,000 feet. Common species, such as the Antarctic cormorant, however, nest near the sea.

Nine of the world's 13 species of albatrosses nest in the southern hemisphere and are common in the Antarctic region. Essentially oceanic seabirds, albatrosses are magnificent fliers. These birds cover great expanses of the globe using relatively little muscular effort, as their long, slim wings enable them to ride air currents for hours on end.

Albatrosses usually mate for life, which can be as long as 50 years. Typical of the larger species is the wandering albatross, which reproduces—the female laying a single egg—only once every two years. The young are fed by the parents for four to five weeks; as winter nears, however, the adults are forced to leave the young (who do not leave the nest until the following spring) while they go to sea, looking for food.

Unlike the wandering albatross, the sooty albatross is a relatively small, yet very handsome bird. Mating pairs of sooty albatrosses isolate themselves from other birds, nesting on the jagged rocks of cliffs which the water off several Antarctic islands.

Some albatrosses have remarkable adaptations, as is the case of juvenile black-browed and grey-headed albatrosses. When their parents are not able to defend them, the juveniles ward off potential predators by spraying a repulsive, foul-smelling oil into the air—directed at their attackers—which serves as a repellent.

The lack of land birds is not surprising, given the barren state and harsh conditions of the Antarctic continent. In order to try to escape the rigors imposed by the difficult conditions to the south, species such as kelp gulls, larger skuas, and sheathbills nest on the Antarctic Peninsula, an extension of land well north of the South Pole, where conditions are less harsh.

Both the McCormick Great Skua and Lonnbergs Great Skua prefer to nest near colonies of penguins. In addition to being great aerial pirates, these skuas prey upon penguin eggs and juvenile birds.

The Antarctic penguins, which include emperors, Adèlies, rockhoppers, and kings, are among the more fascinating bird species found in the continent. Huge colonies of penguins, often numbering tens of thousands, thrive throughout the Antarctic. Penguins are well adapted for the rigors of Antarctic life. Their wings have evolved into fins or flippers, and their feet are webbed—a feature which helps them serve as modified fins when swimming. Penguins have a thick layer of fat which provides additional warmth and a source of energy, and their dense feathers are smooth and thick at the base, supplying added warmth.

With the exception of royal and emperor penguins, all penguins build nests. Eggs are incubated by both parents, many of whom mate for life. As a general rule, penguins only come onto land to incubate their eggs and to raise their young. They spend the rest of their lives in the water, where relatively little is known about their habits. They are, however, superb swimmers, traveling great distances to feed and then return to their nests.

Once threatened to the point of extinction by chemical pesticides weakening the shells of their eggs, brown pelicans (*Pelecanus occidentalis*) have made an encouraging comeback. (FOLLOWING PAGES) Like thick-billed murres, common or thin-billed murres breed in huge coastal colonies on rocky cliffs and ledges. When the young are about half-grown, they jump 30 to 50 feet off the cliffs into the water to join their parents.

Colonial breeders, these double-crested cormorants (*Phalacrocorax auritus*) are the most widespread of North American cormorants, ranging from the Aleutians, throughout North America, and down to Cuba in both marine and freshwater areas.

Razorbills (*Alca torda*) are colonial breeders that are gregarious throughout the year. In flight, they fly fast and low over the waters of the North Atlantic and North Pacific, where they feed.

Fairy terns (*Sterna nereis*) inhabit some coastal areas of Australia and New Zealand. Colonial breeders, they are exclusively marine birds, inhabiting both coastal and inshore waters.

The courtship rituals of many birds, like the pair of wandering albatrosses (*Diomedea exulans*) pictured here, involve elaborate displays and exaggerated posturing. Albatrosses usually mate for life.

(ABOVE AND BELOW) Atlantic puffins (*Fratercula arctica*), one of three species of puffins, are found throughout the North Atlantic. They nest in small colonies, breeding in burrows along rocky coasts from Greenland to Maine.

Despite their chunky build, puffins are good fliers as well as excellent swimmers and divers. Using their wings for propulsion underwater, puffins pursue a variety of fish, mollusks, and crustaceans.

Horned puffins (*Fratercula corniculata*) inhabit sea cliffs and small rocky or grass-covered islands in the North Pacific. Like the Atlantic and tufted puffins, these nonmigratory birds are colonial breeders.

31

(PRECEDING PAGES, ABOVE AND BELOW) Found only in the equatorial islands of the Galàpagos off the west coast of Ecuador, marine iguanas (*Amblyrhynchus cristatus*) feed on algae that grows on rocks close to shore. Most enter the surprisingly cold waters only once a day, for an hour or less. Between dives, they bask in the equatorial sun to increase their body heat. Marine iguanas often gather in tight groups or pile up on top of each other to conserve body heat. Their fierce looks belie their shy and docile nature.

All sea turtles bury their eggs in depressions they dig on sandy tropical beaches. Hatchlings, like this newborn leatherback turtle, are extremely vulnerable to predation from birds and fish, especially sharks.

Mudskippers (*Periophthalmus*) are one of the few fishes that remain on mudflats while other fish depart with the receding tide. As long as their gills remain moist, mudskippers can stay out of water for extended periods of time.

(PRECEDING PAGES) Like most pinnipeds, Northern sea lions do haul out onto land, but they rarely stray far from water. Seals and sea lions possess a thick layer of blubber which helps keep them warm in water, but the threat of overheating poses a real danger on land. (ABOVE) Like all mammals, harbor seals breathe air, are warm-blooded, have a backbone, have hair or fur, and nurse their young. The mammary glands are tucked under the fore-flippers. (BELOW) Ranging from Alaska to the Baja peninsula in Mexico, harbor seals (*Phoca vitulina*) are easily identified by their small size, chunky build, small fore-flippers, and their light coat, covered with dark spots. As a rule, they tend to be more wary of intruding divers than do many species of seals.

Elephant seals (*Mirounga leonina*) are known for the large bulbous snout possessed by the males of the species. Adult males are the largest of all seals, reaching a length of up to 16 feet and weighing as much as 5,000 pounds.

(PAGE 40) Lobsters are common residents of tropical and temperate reefs around the world, but fishing pressure has reduced populations to alarmingly low levels in many areas. It takes some species up to seven years to reach sexual maturity. (PAGE 41) Lobsters are primarily nocturnal and usually prefer to seek refuge in caves and crevices during the day. (ABOVE) Most California spiny lobsters (*Palinurus*) are one- to two-feet-long and weigh between one and three pounds, but the largest specimen ever documented was an astonishing three-feet-long and weighed 35 pounds. Scientists estimated the lobster to be more than 100-years-old.

Pelagic red crabs are usually found free-swimming in the open sea, but at times, these crabs invade coastal waters by the millions. Reasons for the invasions are unknown, but some scientists suspect that reproduction is the central issue.

Hermit crabs protect themselves by crawling into the shell of a deceased snail, which becomes a permanent mobile home.

When danger threatens, the crab retreats inside of the shell and later extends its stalked eyes to determine if the danger has passed.

Octopi are secretive animals, preferring to hide during the day. Any crack, crevice, or shell will do as a protective shelter.

Sally lightfoot crabs (*Grapsus grapsus*) acquire their name from their habit of skipping lightly across short stretches of water. These crabs move in nimble fashion in their realm on rocky beaches where they feed on algae and detritus. (BELOW) Nocturnal feeders as a rule, octopi are extremely efficient predators. They use any or all of their eight sucker-bearing arms to capture prey, which they then paralyze with secreted toxins. This octopus has just captured a tuna crab which can be seen by a close look at the octopus' sac-like mantle.

The goose barnacles pictured above are usually associated with mussel populations. Named for their long "goose-neck-like" stems, they are the species that so often cover pier pilings. In the 1500's, a prominent Greek naturalist actually maintained that geese hatched from these barnacles. Science has come a long way, indeed!

(BELOW) Barnacles feed by extending their feather-like feet up into the water column and then sweeping their feet through the water in an attempt to catch tiny food particles. (OPPOSITE) Acorn barnacles are often found on exposed, current-swept rocks on open ocean seamounts, not close to shore in the intertidal zone.

Nudibranchs are mollusks who have lost their shells. Meaning "naked gills" in Latin, the term "nudibranch" refers to their exposed respiratory organs, which are the flower-like projections in the species pictured here.

Many species of scallops cement themselves to the substrate as adults. However, the species pictured above is free-swimming, propelling itself with forceful jets of water created by rapidly closing its shells.

The blue spots in the mantle of the scallop pictured here are its eyes. Surprisingly well-developed in scallops, the eyes sense the presence of potential predators by noting changes in light intensity.

Brittle stars are echinoderms, so named for their brittle arms, which tend to break off at the tiniest disturbance. The arms can usually be regenerated.

Giant red urchins (*Strongylocentrotus drobachensis*) play vital roles in the ecology of California reef communities, feeding on a variety of algaes, including the holdfasts of giant kelp plants. Sea otters and some fishes prey on the urchins.

Ochre stars are common residents of many temperate reef communities. Their coloration varies widely, ranging from yellow to orange, blue, brown, purple, and red. These sea stars prefer to feed on mussels.

Spectacularly colored file shells are commonly found in many Caribbean reef communities. They are much more active and easier to locate at night, when they leave the deep recesses of the reef to feed.

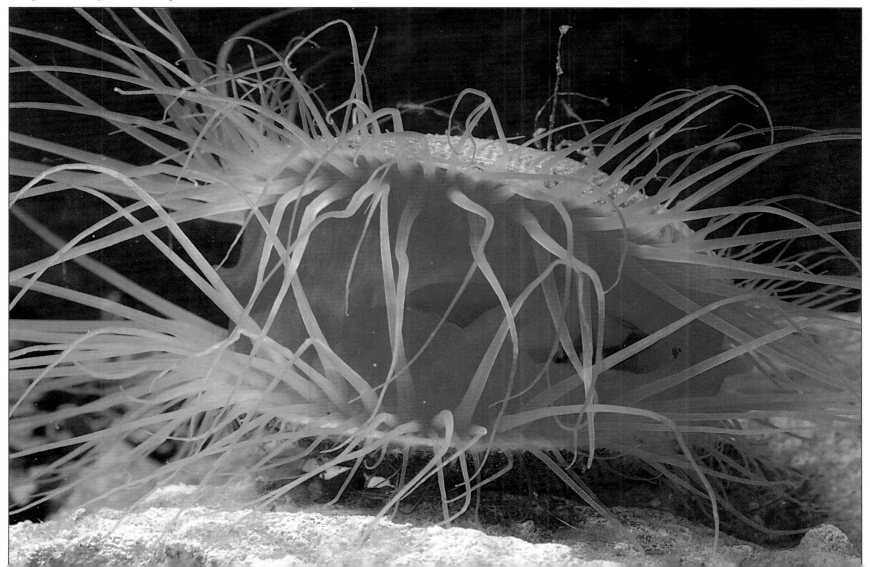

These marine catfish (*Plotusus anguillaris*) are among the most dangerous fishes found in the shallow, coastal waters of Indo-Pacific reefs. Their dorsal and pectoral fins have venom glands capable of inflicting extremely painful wounds.

Sand dollars are echinoderms, flattened relatives of sea urchins. They do not possess the long spines found in urchins because the spines would be broken off by the shifting sands on the bottom where sand dollars live.

Scenes like this jewfish being accompanied by one or more remoras are quite common. Sometimes the remoras swim alongside the jewfish, and sometimes the remoras attach themselves to the jewfish by using a sucker-like disc on the tops of their heads.

Flatfishes, like this turbot, are masters of camouflage. Experiments have shown that they can quickly change their coloration to match even the most subtle changes in their surroundings by expanding or contracting specialized cells called iridocytes and chromatophores.

Humpback whales utilize a variety of feeding techniques, including lunging and "bubble-netting." In lunge feeding, the whales rush up from deep water with mouths agape. When bubble-netting, humpbacks circle below their prey and, as they rise toward the surface, the whales gently expel air, which rises in bubble columns that form a screen or "net" around their entrapped prey.

point of scientific debate. Various theories suggest that breaching is: part of an elaborate splay, of assistance in dislodging parasites; it feels good.

Killer whales (*Orcinus orca*) propel themselves at speed of approximately 30 miles per hour when building up speed to breach.

...i s tail," a maneuver called "sparing or spy-hopping." Exactly why whales spy-hop is not known.
...orient with coastal landmarks, but other scientists claim their vision in air is too poor.

(ABOVE AND BELOW) Tightly packed schools of swirling barracuda are common sights on many Indo-Pacific reefs. Among the fastest of swimmers, barracuda are major predators in coral reef communities. Their fusiform shape helps them reduce drag and greatly enhances their effort to outswim their prey. (OPPOSITE) Almost all schooling fishes, like the snappers pictured here, face into currents to look for food and weakened potential prey. Floating helplessly in a current is a distinct sign of vulnerability.

Horn sharks (Family *Heterodontidae*) are restricted in the habitats in which they can survive because their favorite prey consists of a variety of mollu⟨⟩s, crustaceans, echinoderms, and small fish, found close to shore in temperate and tropical seas.

Carpet sharks (Family *Parascylliidae*) lead a fairly sluggish existence, feeding on the bottom in shallow water. Though these animals will never be th⟨⟩ st⟨⟩ of a Hollywood thriller, in a purely scientific sense, they are every bit as much of a shark as are great whites and any other species.

obesus) are extremely common on tropical reefs in the Indo-Pacific. Like many species of sharks they are primarily
[da]y they often rest in caves, under ledges, or on sand bottoms. (BELOW) Vision in sharks is not well understood, although it
[spe]cies to species. Sharks that live in clear, shallow water are generally believed to have better vision than species that live in
[how] much sharks rely on vision, as compared to other senses, is also believed to vary greatly from one species to the next.

providing a home for many marine species like the bright orange garibaldi pictured here, giant kelp is commercially harvested by ucts are used in over 70 commercial and household products.

crab pictured here, spend the majority of their lives floating with small masses of Sargassum, which provide both food and shelter.

eaweed that is known as Sargassum support a remarkably diverse community of marine animals, including hydroids, bryozoans, =), shrimp, crabs, worms, and an array of fishes.

The range of giant kelpfish (*Heterostichus rostratus*) extends from the southern tip of the Baja peninsula of Mexico to British Columbia, Canada. They are fairly common in kelp forest communities, but their expertise in matters of camouflage makes them a special prize for observant photographers. (OPPOSITE) Stromatolites, such as this one found in the Bahamas, could easily be mistaken for stones on the ocean floor. In fact, it is one of the oldest living life forms, dating back to the Pre-Cambrian Age.

The family of fishes known as surfperches are viviparous, meaning they bear live young. Breeding occurs during summer, but fertilization does not take place until the following spring. The female stores the sperm separate from the eggs.

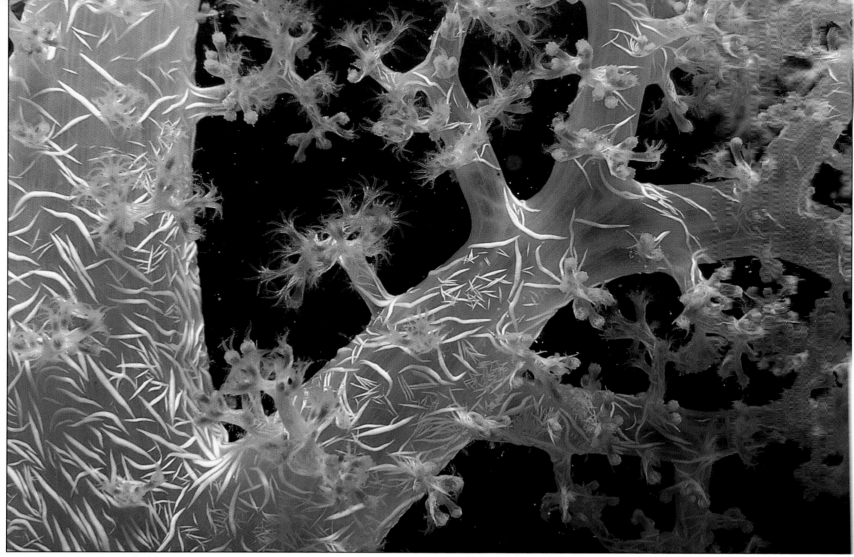

Delicate soft corals occur in a variety of colors. However, divers do not see warm colors at great depths, like the pink in this soft coral, unless they carry an underwater light and hold it close to their subjects.

Soft corals are considered to be colonial, because the individual polyps share a common skeleton that consists of a rubber-like mass that is laced with calcerous spicules. These help give the skeleton some rigidity.

(PRECEDING) This yellow soft coral is actively feeding. The polyps are extended out into the water column in an effort to capture particles of food that are floating in the current.

Some hard corals like the brain coral (ABOVE) thrive in shallow water where there is a lot of surge, wave action, and current.

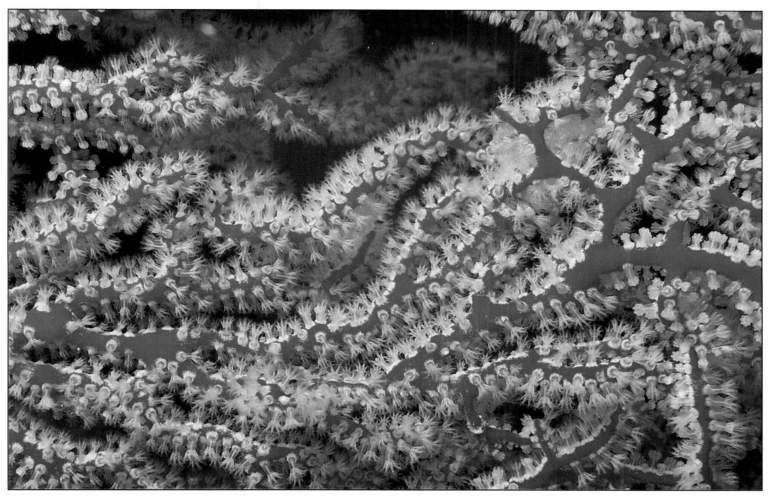

Corals are stationary animals and depend upon water movement to bring them food. Coral polyps are armed with stinging nematocysts and a layer of sticky mucus to help them snare their prey.

Colonial animals, soft corals like this sea fan are often mistaken for plants by novice divers.

(PRECEDING) While sea anemones are found in waters throughout the world, symbiotic clownfishes are only found in anemones that live in the Red Sea and Indo-Pacific. (ABOVE) Many clownfishes are hatched from eggs that are attached to the base of anemones. These fish quickly acclimate to their hosts by creating a layer of mucus that inhibits the stinging nematocysts of the anemone.

When anemones capture their food, they use their tentacles to take the food (the small flatfish pictured here) to their centrally located mouths.

Fish the size of clownfish—like the butterfly fish pictured here—are often stung and killed by anemones.

Anemones can reproduce sexually, but they also display a variety of innovative methods of asexual reproduction. They might simply split into two halves, or, in some cases, as they move they leave fragments of tissue which develop into adult anemones.

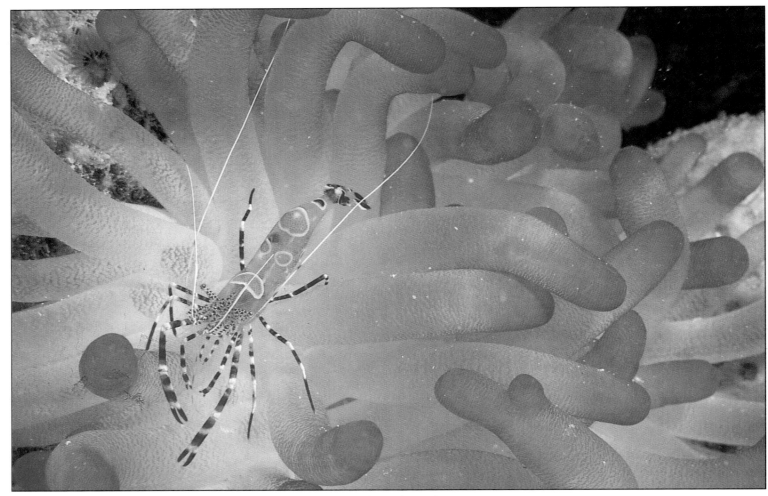

A variety of shrimp and crabs are commonly found living in a symbiotic relationship with anemones.

A variety of spectacularly colored *Telia* anemones are among the most stunning invertebrates in the temperate waters off western North America.

The color patterns, leaf-like appendages, and shape of fishes such as this three-spined scorpionfish help them blend into their surroundings, making them less obvious to potential prey and predators alike.

Typical of all scorpionfishes, the leaf scorpionfish is a relatively poor swimmer. Sharp, toxic spines atop an erect dorsal fin serve as a defense mechanism that wards off predators.

The California scorpionfish (*Scorpaena guttata*) provides a classic case study illustrating the need to identify wildlife with precise scientific nomenclature, denoting their genus and species. This fish is commonly called a sculpin, as are 44 other species in California alone. However, despite its common name, the California scorpionfish is not even a member of the same family of fishes as the other 44 species commonly called sculpin.

All groupers begin their lives as females. Those that survive produce eggs, and then, amazing as it might seem, change sex and become functioning males. (OPPOSITE) Colorful sea fans sit high on the reef as schools of fish swarm above in a typical coral reef scene.

Clams are those members of the mollusk family which are bivalves.

The colors in the mantles of giant clams range from iridescent blues and greens to drab brown. The vivid colors are mostly due to the presence of high concentrations of symbiotic zooanthellae algae in the tissue of the mantle.

Giant Pacific *Tridachna* clams can exceed four feet in height and weigh more than 500 pounds.

Feather stars, often called crinoids, are the most ancient class of echinoderms. Many specimens are brightly colored in a wide range of hues, while others are solid black to brown.

Sea snakes are common in the Indo-Pacific, but none are found in Caribbean or Atlantic waters, probably because they never succeeded in getting around the cold waters at the southern tip of Africa.

(OPPOSITE) Coneys are common members of the grouper family. They tend to hover close to the bottom and do not stray far from the protection of the reef. (ABOVE) Lionfish are among the most ornate fishes found in coral reef communities. When hunting, lionfish usually herd their prey into pockets in the reef before lunging quickly, rather than using their toxic dorsal or pectoral spines. (FOLLOWING PAGES) Snappers are very common in tropical waters and in many places are the most important food fish. Snappers tend to school, and most are nocturnal carnivores that feed on a mix of crustaceans.

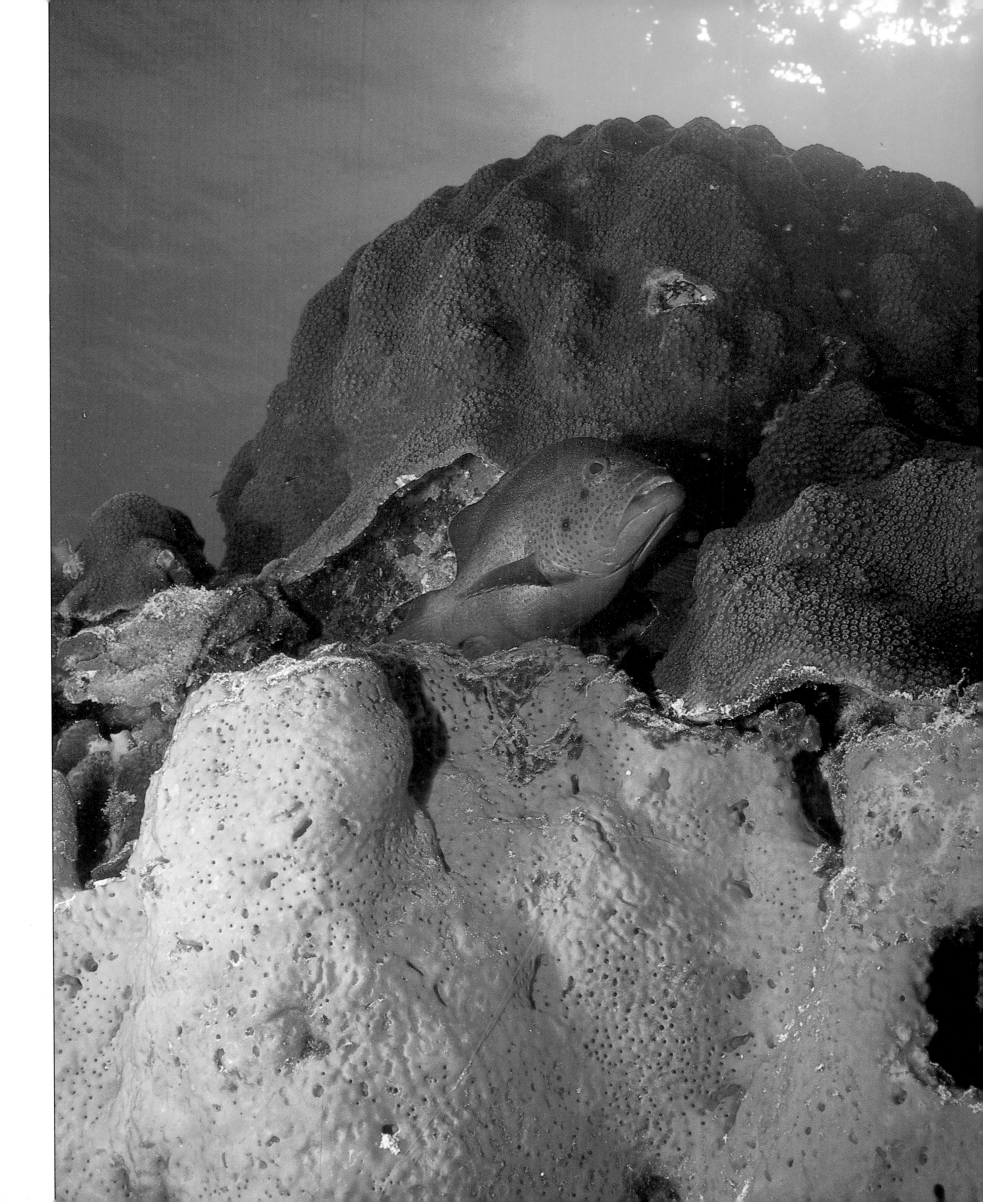

(OPPOSITE) Puffers often hide in recesses in the reef but, when feeling threatened in exposed areas, they will rely on their ability to inflate and erect sharp spines to protect themselves, rather than swimming for cover. (ABOVE) Scientists speculate that fish use patterns and colors in a variety of ways such as helping to identify their species, to enhance their ability to tell males from females, to distinguish juveniles from adults, and to confuse predators.

A crown blenny, found off the coast of Baja California.

Closely related to squid and octopi, cuttlefish are among the most advanced mollusks. Excellent swimmers, cuttlefish are predaceous carnivores, feeding primarily upon fish. (OPPOSITE) Even the cherry red sponges pictured here appear drab brown to purple at depth. Underwater photographers use strobes or flash units inside of watertight housings to paint colors into their images.

Peacock flounder (*Bothus unatus*) are a type of flatfish. As adults, they often lie buried in the sand with only their eyes exposed. Like the larvae of other flatfishes, the position of the eyes in the larvae of peacock flounder resembles most other fishes with one eye on each side of the head. As the larvae matures, one eye migrates over so that both eyes are on one side of the head by the time the fish is ready to settle out of the plankton into a bottom-dwelling existence.

The king or passer angel is a very common reef fish in waters from Mexico's Sea of Cortez to the Galápagos Islands. Typical of most angel fishes, adults are often seen in pairs.

Growing to a length of about 18 inches, queen angels are common in Caribbean reef communities. Queen angels feed mostly on sponges but also eat some algae, hydroids, tunicates, and bryozoans.

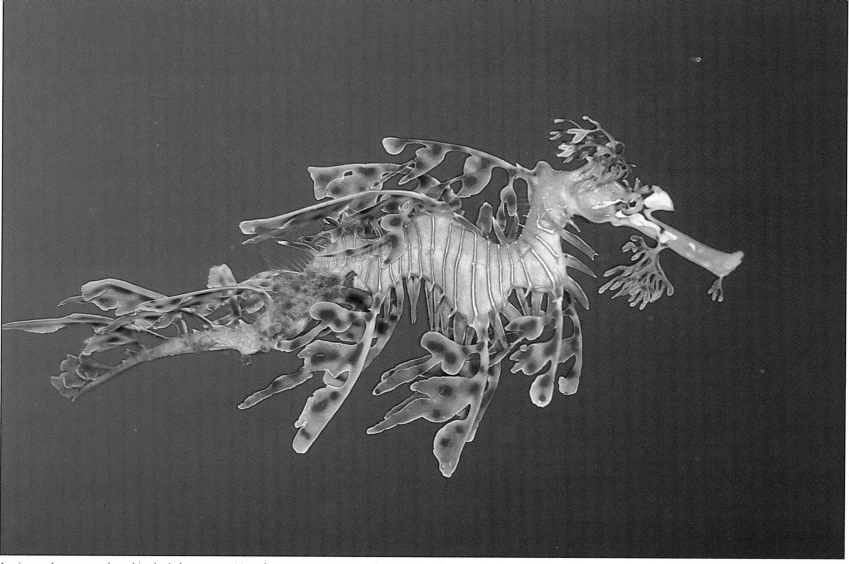

Leafy sea dragons are found in the kelp communities of temperate seas in south Australia. They are closely related to seahorses and, like seahorses, the male carries and protects the unhatched eggs. Note the purple cluster of eggs high on the underside of the tail of this male.

In seahorses, the male of the species has a pouch much like that of a female kangaroo. As the female lays her eggs the male fertilizes them, and the eggs are deposited in the male's pouch. The male guards the eggs until they hatch.

Lacking both pelvic and caudal fins, seahorses are comparatively weak swimmers. They rely on camouflage, their ability to hide, their rigid body, and their bony armor as their chief means of protection.

When food sources (usually small crustaceans) float by, seahorses quickly suck them into their tube-like mouths.

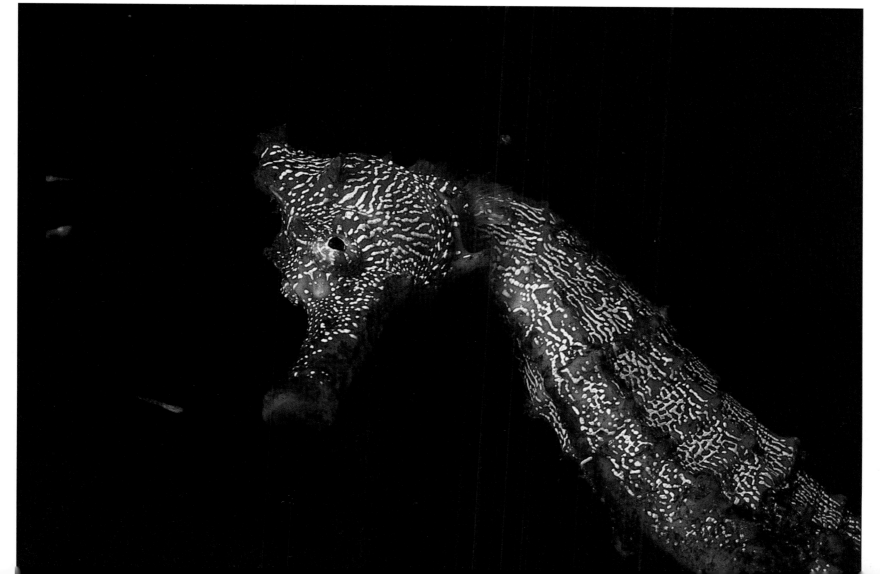

Some fishes are described as pickers, meaning they feed by "picking" or sucking suspended particles of food out of the water column. Pickers often disappear into the protective confines of the reef at night, only to appear in the water column again with the rising sun. (BELOW) Having the same reproductive biology and sharing many common physiological characteristics, parrotfishes are closely related to wrasses. In both families, a "supermale" maintains a harem of females with whom he mates in separate sessions. (OPPOSITE) Excellent in their effort to mimic branched corals, trumpetfishes often hang upside down amongst the corals in order to camouflage themselves.

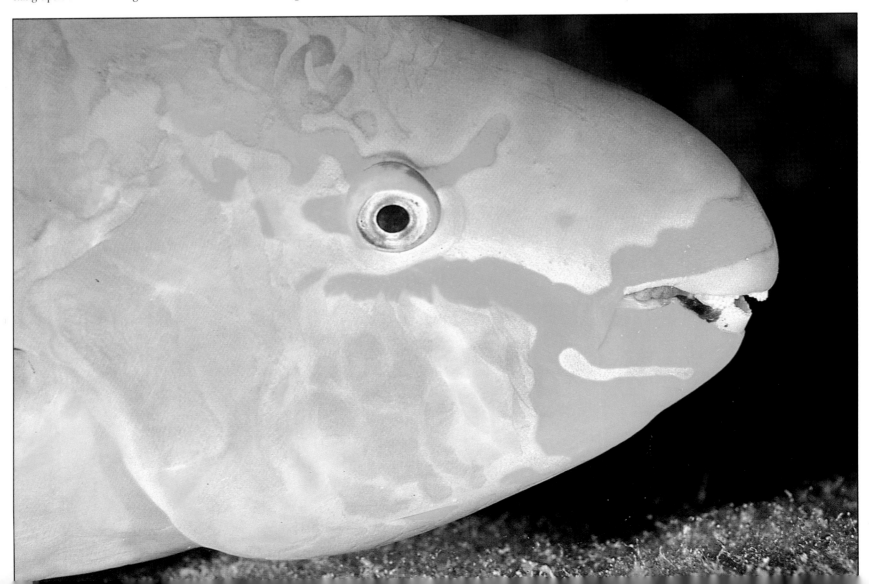

(PRECEDING PAGE) Primarily nocturnal hunters, squirrelfish are often found suspended in the water column near the entrances to caves, or under ledges and overhangs during the day. (ABOVE) Swarming about in constantly moving schools, small fishes such as these Anthias confuse predators by filling their visual field and making it difficult to select a single target.

When feeling threatened, pufferfish can inflate themselves to twice their normal size by swallowing water. Puffers, known as *fugu* in Japan, are highly prized food-fish, but some species can cause death if improperly prepared.

Colorful rope sponges are commonly found on walls and drop-offs in Caribbean reef communities. Rope sponges appear in a variety of colors from bright red to olive green.

Like most moray eels, the California moray (*Gymnothorax mordax*) appears far more vicious than it is. Reaching lengths close to six feet, these eels are rather shy residents in rocky reefs in southern California and the northern Baja peninsula.

Moray eels are common residents of tropical and temperate reef communities, where they prey on small fish, octopi, squid, and crustaceans. This species was photographed in New Zealand.

Protected by its behavioral identification code, which is composed of a combination of color and movement, a busy cleaner wrasse goes to work cleaning a moray eel. The wrasse and eel have a symbiotic relationship, further defined as "mutualism" in which both animals benefit and neither is harmed. The reasons for symbiotic associations usually involve protection, a source of food, cleaning, or transportation. In the case of this wrasse and moray eel, the wrasse gains food and protection by the mere presence of the eel who is not likely to harm a cleaner. The eel benefits from the cleaning as the wrasse rids the moray of parasites, bacteria, and dead tissue.

Morays are generally solitary, but it is not uncommon to encounter several eels peering out of the same crevice or to have eels gather in groups when being fed by divers.

Disk jellies, such as the ones pictured on this page, enjoy worldwide distribution. (OPPOSITE) Jellyfish, known as *Pelagia noctilucu*, are found off the coast of Puerto Rico.

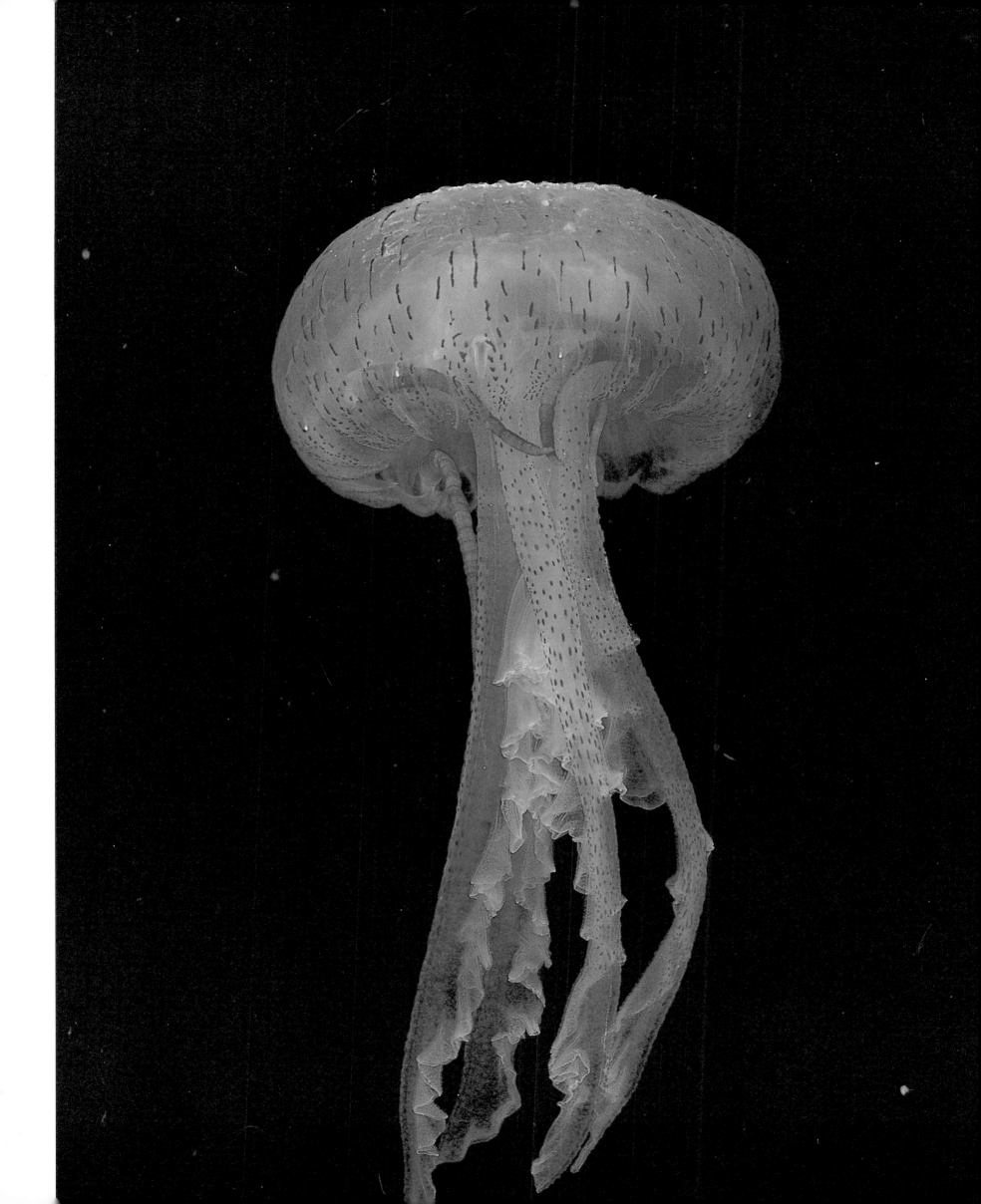

The spectacular breaching by California gray whales is often repeated as many as 10 times in succession within a two- or three-minute span. During the act of breaching, gray whales often spin in the air before crashing and splashing back into the sea. (THIS PAGE AND PRECEDING PAGES) Common dolphins (*Delphinus delphi*) generally travel in huge pods of a thousand or more. Constantly leaping clear of the water, they are very active animals. Common dolphins will dive to depths of close to 1,000 feet to feed on lanternfishes and squid.

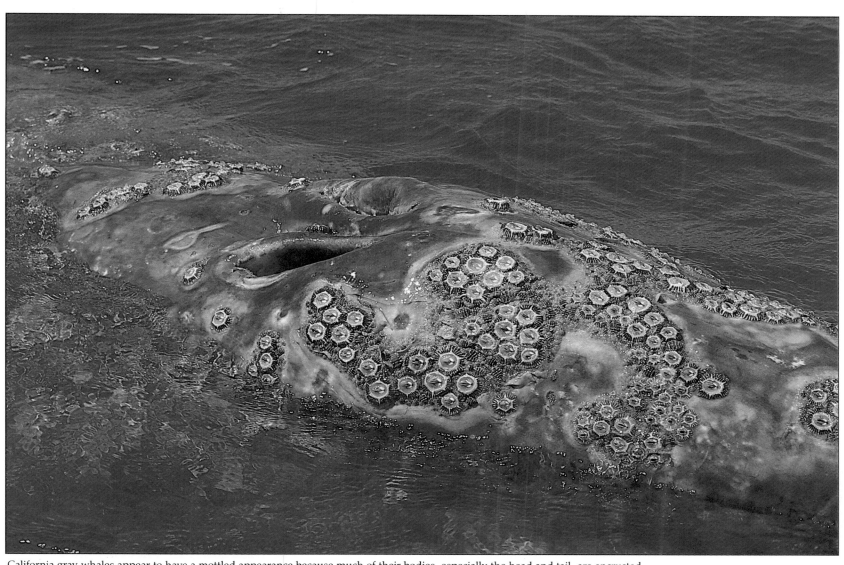

California gray whales appear to have a mottled appearance because much of their bodies, especially the head and tail, are encrusted with barnacles. Clusters of tiny crustaceans, known as whale lice, living on the barnacle colonies and the whale's skin often create orange-colored patches of skin.

Scientists suspect that one of the main reasons for the evolutionary success enjoyed by sharks stems from the fact that different species occupy the same niches in different environments. The oceanic whitetip (*Carcharhinus longimanus*), pictured here, occupies the same open-ocean predatory niche in tropical seas as the blue shark (*Prionace glauca*) does in temperate waters.

The pilot fish (*Naucrates ductor*) which accompany blue sharks and other open-ocean animals, do so in the hopes of scavenging a free meal from left-overs. Pilot fish are sometimes found in the stomach content analyses of sharks.

Hammerhead sharks are easily recognizable due to their flattened, laterally extended heads which have a "hammer-like" appearance. The largest of the nine species of hammerheads is the great hammerhead, which is documented to 18 feet.

Great white sharks are countershaded, being dark on the top and light on the bottom. This color pattern helps them blend in with lightly hued surface waters when viewed from below, and dark reef bottoms when the sharks swim overhead. Countershading is a big advantage for predators and prey alike.

Flying fishes are preyed upon by a variety of larger animals, including billfish, dolphins, and sharks. Their 35 mile-per-hour "flights," which can reach a length of 150 feet for a duration of 13 seconds, are made in an attempt to escape potential predators. (OPPOSITE) Tuna are highly migratory fishes, often traveling great distances in dense schools. Their migrations require a great deal of energy, and some species consume as much as 25 percent of their body weight every day.

Most of the 43 known species of flying fishes are found offshore, over deep water. Little is known about their natural histories.

Like most stingrays, southern stingrays (*Dasyatis americana*) are found in near-shore habitats and bays. Despite the potentially dangerous tail spines possessed by these rays, divers can safely approach to within inches. At some dive resorts, "wild" stingrays are hand-fed by divers on a regular basis.

Eagle rays are superb swimmers, providing a special thrill for envious divers. They are usually encountered as solitary animals or in small groups. Eagle rays have rows of grinding teeth, used to feed on clams, oysters, crabs, lobsters, shrimp, and snails.

Cow rays (*Rhinoptera*) are often seen in large schools. When near the surface, these rays will often leap several feet out of the water, doing a series of acrobatic flips, turns, and twists while airborne.

Once quite common in tropical seas, all species of sea turtles have experienced severe reductions in population, due to overfishing and overuse of their nesting areas.

A protected species in many parts of the world, green turtles (*Chelonia mydas*) can be seen in the Florida Keys and the northern Hawaiian islands, where they breed and nest. Green turtles have a black carapace, or shell. Their name is derived from their green-colored fatty tissues.

The turtle-grass beds needed for survival by hawksbill turtles (*Eretmochelys impricata*) have been substantially reduced by pollution.
The turtles' beautiful shells, made from a number of overlapping horny plates, were the original source of tortoiseshell jewelry for
which many turtles were killed. The fish pictured here is a French angel.

Octopi are active predators. They use their well-developed eyes to see potential predators, and their sucker-bearing tentacles to catch them. (BELOW) Octopi are capable of rapidly changing their coloration. The color red is thought to indicate a feeling like anger or fear. If threatened or pursued, octopi can release ink from an internal sac to distract or confuse predators. The ink also works as an anesthetic, dulling the olfactory senses of predators such as moray eels.

An octopus swims by means of jet propulsion in which water is forced through a flexible siphon in its mantle. This siphon can be aimed in any direction.

Octopi are considered to be the most intelligent of the invertebrates. They possess a large sac-like head, have complex brains, and eyes not unlike our own.

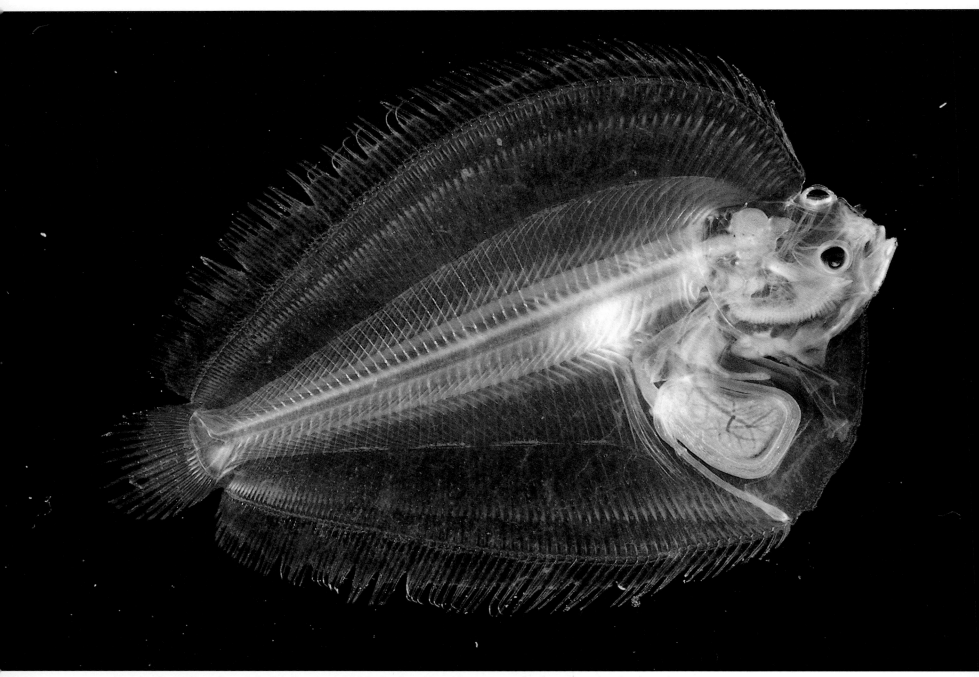

(PRECEDING PAGES) Camouflage through body coloration is highly developed in midwater invertebrates, such as this Caridean shrimp (*Parapasiphaea*). The red color of *Parapasiphaea* reflects virtually no blue-green light, the dominant color of bioluminescence, which is the major source of light in the midwater environment. *Parapasiphaea* feeds on other small shrimp and invertebrates. In the claw of this shrimp is a small mysid (*Eucopia*). The white tuft on the head of the shrimp is a sporozoan infection. (ABOVE) Typical of many species of fishes who live their adult lives as benthic creatures, Dover sole (*MicrostomusApacificus*) are pelagic in their larval stage. At 1.5 inches, they are uncommonly large for post-larval fishes, and can spend up to a year swimming in the open ocean before settling to the bottom to start life as juvenile fishes. Adult Dover sole live along the continental slope to depths of 1200 meters. They are an important commercial resource in the offshore ground fishery.

Cystisoma is an amphipod, living in the dim light of the mesopelagic environment. Its size ranges to six inches in length. Due to difficulties of seeing, many of the organisms that live there have large eyes with high light-gathering power. The large orangish-colored eyes of *Cystisoma* occupy most of the head region, and are arranged in diffuse plates which look upward. This arrangement makes the amphipod less visible to predators, since the rest of the animal is completely transparent. The animal is also better able to see prey species silhouetted against the dim background light from the surface.

Midwater jellyfish such as *Periphyllina* are some of the most effective predators of the open ocean. Almost neutrally buoyant, these jellyfish extend their tentacles in net-like fashion as they drift slowly downward waiting for prey. Once contact with prey is made, stinging cells (nematocysts) along the tentacles fire dart-like harpoons that paralyze and stun the unsuspecting victim. Most midwater jellyfish are small; however, some species can grow to a meter or more in diameter.

These barnacles (*Lepas fasicularis*), which drift near the surface of the open ocean, make their own float instead of attaching to some other object. The cement which barnacles produce to attach themselves to floating objects is modified in this species to produce a gas-filled float, similar in structure to Styrofoam.

Anglerfish, such as this Caulophrisid, are common to the mesopelagic (or deep-sea) zone. The appendage protruding from its head acts as a lure for unsuspecting fish.

The gaping jaws of this Pacific fang tooth (*Anaplogaster cornuta*) are terrifying in close-up.

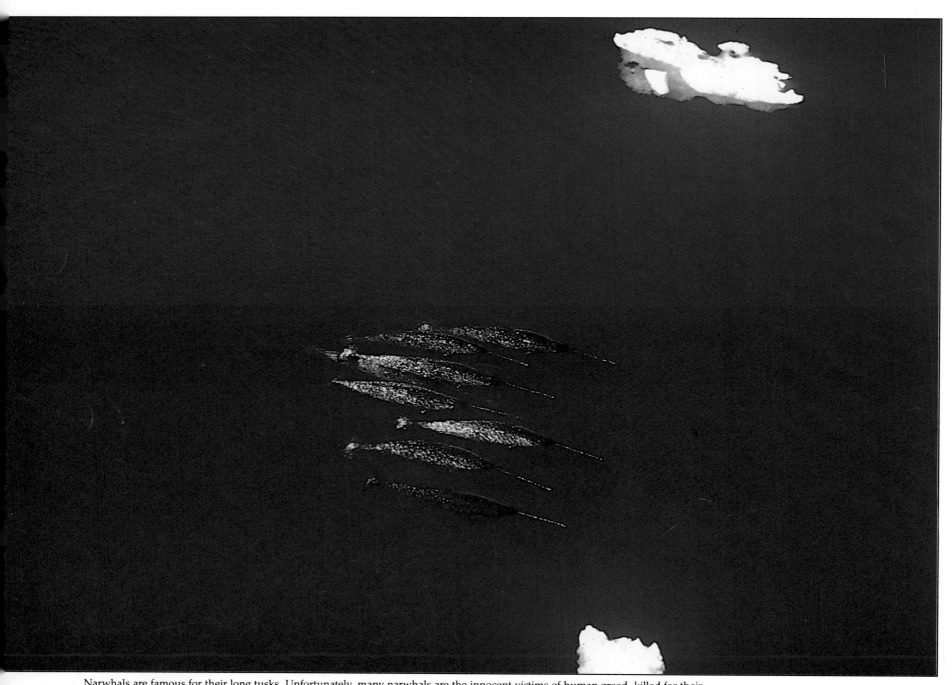

Narwhals are famous for their long tusks. Unfortunately, many narwhals are the innocent victims of human greed, killed for their tusks to support an illegal ivory trade.

White whales (*Delphinapterus leucas*), also commonly called beluga whales, are very gregarious. They are often found in pods of hundreds or even thousands.

(PRECEDING PAGES) Humpback whales are most easily recognized by their extremely long pectoral flippers. Another identifying characteristic, pictured here, is the pronounced dorsal fin, located about two-thirds of the way down the body. (ABOVE) When humpback whales dive, or sound, their tail flukes are raised high into the air, showing the scalloped edge as well as the white underside. Among other reasons, humpbacks dive to seek small schooling fishes and krill.

The tail of a blue whale (*Balaenoptera musculus*). Blue whales, the largest life forms on earth, rely on plankton—one of the smallest— for sustenance.

Beluga whales have large layers of fat and are very well-adapted for their cold-water existence. They tend to gather in shallow waters near river mouths and bays, where they raise their calves.

Beluga whales' primary predators are orcas (killer whales) and polar bears.

(PRECEDING PAGES) Walrus colonies consist of a large number of individuals that are dominated by huge males. The colonies are normally found near stretches of shallow water, where the walruses can find plenty of their favorite food, clams. (ABOVE) Of all their senses, only the sense of smell is well-developed in walruses. These mammals rely on their smell primarily to detect potential predators.

Very agile in water, harp seals (*Pagophilus groenlandicus*), like other seals, find travelling on land to be difficult. Their terrestrial gait makes one think of a large caterpillar.

Leopard seals (*Hydrurga leptonyx*) prey heavily upon Adélie penguins, especially during the penguin's breeding season. The seals patrol ice floes for unsuspecting Adélies.

Even though Adélie penguins appear awkward on land, they are more agile than the seals, and many escape predation. Those penguins who do not get away from the seals are shaken, then thrown through the air with enough force to tear their skin and feathers off in one tidy package.

Harp seals breed on the shores of Newfoundland and Greenland. The young pups have a dense white fur for the first two weeks of their lives, which is especially prized by hunters.

The hooded seal pictured here is a male with an inflated septum, an organ used in vocalizations and communications. Only the males possess the enlarged septum.

(PRECEDING PAGES) Having no fixed lair, polar bears are constant travelers. Seeking the shelter of ravines or gorges only during the coldest times, polar bears are generally solitary creatures, and male and female only gather together during a short mating season. (ABOVE) Although polar bears do spend plenty of time on land, they are excellent swimmers and can easily maintain a speed of six miles per hour.

Well-camouflaged for their predatory life on land, polar bears can often approach their intended prey quite closely without detection. Only their black nose and eyes stand out as non-white body parts against the ice and snow.

Brown skuas (*Atharacta antartica*) are notorious for pirating food from shags, petrels, and gulls by harassing them until they regurgitate their food. Brown skuas mate freely with South Polar skuas, producing hybrid chicks.

Brown skuas show no fear of humans and fiercely defend their breeding territories.

Albatrosses are the largest of all sea birds. Known for their great soaring ability, they visit land only for breeding purposes. The light-mantled sooty albatrosses (*Phoebetria pallebrata*) seen here are found throughout southern oceans.

Most albatrosses feed on fish and squid, which they then bring to their nests and regurgitate for their young.

(PRECEDING PAGES) King penguins (*Aptenodytes patagonicas*) breed in large, dense colonies on Antarctic islands. They are unique among penguins in that they breed twice every three years. (ABOVE) King penguins are considered to be quite tame while in breeding colonies and are very easy to approach. When not breeding, they are found many miles out to sea over deep water. (OPPOSITE) Penguins only stay on land to hatch and raise their young.

Chinstrap penguins (*Pygosoelis antarctica*) are characterized by the black line under their heads from which they get their name. Excellent climbers, chinstraps sometimes nest several hundred yards above sea level.

154

Adélie penguins (*Pygosoelis adelie*) are the most abundant of all penguins. Excellent swimmers, Adélies can exit the water by jumping to an icy ledge that is as high as six feet above the surface of the sea.

The largest of all penguins, emperor penguins stand over three feet tall. They are capable of diving to a depth of 870 feet, deeper than any other bird. Emperors feed primarily on squid.

Emperor penguins are the only penguins to breed on the Antarctic ice shelf during winter, when the temperature commonly plummets to –40°C. (FOLLOWING PAGES) Penguins appear awkward on land as they move with a combination of waddles and hops. However, in the water their rigid flippers make them graceful swimmers. Penguins exhale before they dive, but dives can last up to six minutes.

Index of Photographers